User Risk:
The Missing Variable in the Risk Management Framework

Dr. James W. Howell, Jr.

A SMARTCIO, LLC BOOK NEVADA

User Risk:
The Missing Variable in the
Risk Management Framework

First edition 2026

Published by SmartCIO, LLC
304 S. Jones Blvd.
Las Vegas, NV 89107
https://www.smartcio.com

ISBN 979-8-9943826-3-9 paperback
ISBN 979-8-9943826-4-6 hardcover
ISBN 979-8-9943826-5-3 ebook
Library of Congress Control Number: 2026919850

Printed in the United States of America

Dedication

To the Authorizing Officials, CIOs, CISOs, and security leaders who sign their names to risk decisions and carry the weight of consequence. May this work strengthen your judgment and sharpen your resolve.

To the cybersecurity professionals who execute the Risk Management Framework each day and recognize its limits. Your discipline sustains trust. This book is written for you.

To the next generation of cybersecurity leaders who will inherit the systems we certify today. May you measure risk with greater clarity, courage, and completeness than we did.

Table of Contents

Introduction

"We cannot continue to authorize systems while accepting risk we cannot measure, compare, or explain."
- Dr. James Howell

A number keeps getting ignored. Every system owner accepts risk based on evidence. You review controls, artifacts, and assessment results. You brief leadership, weigh residual exposure, and sign decisions that carry operational and institutional consequences. The process is familiar, structured, and well defended. Yet one factor rarely receives a score.

The user.

Users interact with systems continuously. They authenticate into environments, approve workflows, configure settings, manipulate data, and make judgment calls under time pressure, often while balancing competing priorities. None of this is disputed. What is rarely examined is how these actions, taken collectively and repeatedly, measurably influence system risk.

In today's complex cybersecurity landscape, User Risk is a critical yet often overlooked variable in the NIST Risk Management Framework (RMF). As a senior cybersecurity executive with over 30 years of experience, I have witnessed the persistent challenges that human behavior poses to system security. This work introduces User Risk as a distinct, measurable category of cybersecurity risk that is not explicitly defined in current RMF publications.

This book explores the nuances of User Risk, a dimension that requires a fresh perspective if we are to safeguard our organizations effectively. It shows the problem exists and proposes practical approaches to incorporating User Risk into existing governance structures. It defines User Risk as a measurable operational variable, explains where current frameworks fall short, and outlines methods organizations can use to improve visibility into how human decisions affect system trust.

Why This Book Exists

Despite advances in frameworks such as NIST Special Publication 800-53, User Risk remains inadequately addressed. Systems may pass assessments, controls may test clean, and assurances may appear strong. Yet, security incidents, frequently attributed to "user error," highlight a fundamental gap in our understanding of risk assessment.

This book bridges that gap by providing an in-depth examination of User Risk as a necessary consideration in any comprehensive security strategy. It defines User Risk as the measurable likelihood that human decision variability degrades system trust, control effectiveness, or mission assurance during operational use.

The Human Element

Variability in Human Judgment is an operational constant that directly influences system outcomes. Consequently, systems are operated under far-from-ideal conditions. Organizations must measure and manage that variability. Recognizing this variability allows organizations to treat User Risk as a measurable factor within system security.

Who This Book Is For

This book is intended for a diverse audience that includes:

- **Authorizing Officials (AOs):** Individuals responsible for making risk acceptance decisions

based on control effectiveness.
- **Chief Information Security Officers (CISOs):** Executives tasked with providing insight into the security posture of their organizations and advocating for necessary changes.
- **Cybersecurity Professionals:** Practitioners who execute the RMF daily and recognize its blind spots regarding human behavior.
- **Future Leaders in Cybersecurity:** Those who are entering the field and will eventually inherit today's security frameworks.

By targeting these key audiences, this book seeks to provoke thoughtful discussion and drive measurable change in how User Risk is approached within the RMF context.

How to Read and Apply This Book

The book is organized into five parts, each building on the last to move from identifying a long-standing gap in cybersecurity governance to proposing a practical framework for addressing it.

- **Part I – The Problem RMF Does Not Measure** introduces the central premise of the book. It examines how the Risk Management Framework rigorously evaluates technical safeguards while leaving Human Judgment largely unmeasured, creating a persistent gap between authorization decisions and real-world security outcomes.
- **Part II – Defining User Risk** establishes User Risk as a measurable operational variable rather than a byproduct of compliance or awareness. It introduces the Operational Trust Model, distinguishes measurement from mitigation, and explains how Human Judgment influences the effectiveness of technical controls during system operation.
- **Part III – Measuring What RMF Cannot See**

explores practical approaches for making User Risk observable. It introduces User Risk Indicators, Behavioral Evidence, and the User Risk Measurement Lifecycle, demonstrating how behavioral observations can complement traditional RMF artifacts and strengthen authorization decisions.

- **Part IV – Operationalizing User Risk** focuses on implementation. It explains how organizations can move beyond awareness toward accountability by integrating User Risk into policy, governance, organizational culture, and performance measurement, providing practical examples of how behavioral evidence can improve Operational Trust.
- **Part V – User Risk in an Uncertain Future** examines why measuring User Risk becomes increasingly important as organizations enter the Zero Epoch. As artificial intelligence, quantum computing, and evolving threat landscapes weaken traditional trust mechanisms, Human Judgment becomes an even more significant factor in preserving Operational Trust and informing future cybersecurity governance.

Key Concepts

The following concepts form the foundation of this book's discussion.

- **User Risk:** User Risk is the measurable likelihood that human decision variability degrades system trust, control effectiveness, or mission assurance during operational use.
- **Operational Trust:** Operational Trust describes the level of confidence that security controls continue to function effectively during real-world system operation, where human decision variability influences how those controls are applied.

- **Control Reliability:** Control Reliability refers to the ability of technical safeguards to enforce security requirements as designed consistently.
- **Behavioral Variability:** Behavioral variability describes the differences in how individuals interpret, prioritize, and apply security procedures when interacting with technical safeguards.
- **Administrative Evidence:** Administrative evidence consists of documentation that demonstrates the completion of required security activities such as training, policy acknowledgment, or procedural compliance.
- **Behavioral Evidence:** Behavioral evidence reflects observable actions taken by users during operational system use that influence the effectiveness of implemented security controls.
- **Risk Visibility:** Risk visibility refers to the ability of an organization to observe, evaluate, and compare factors that influence security outcomes.
- **User Risk Indicators:** User Risk Indicators are observable behaviors or decision patterns that suggest the potential for human actions to influence control effectiveness during operational use.

Understanding these concepts provides the foundation for examining how variability in human decision-making influences operational cybersecurity outcomes and why User Risk remains largely unmeasured in many security evaluation processes.

This book uses the RMF as the primary analytical reference point. RMF is widely used across the United States federal and defense environments and provides a structured process for evaluating system risk through defined security controls and authorization decisions. Other governance frameworks address cybersecurity risk differently, but the structural issue this book examines is not unique to RMF. Because RMF provides a disciplined structure for documenting system risk, it offers a useful lens for examining how User Risk influences security outcomes.

As you engage with this book, I encourage you to reflect on your organization's current practices and consider how the principles of User Risk can enhance your approach to security. By prioritizing the human element, we can build more resilient systems that adapt not just to technology but also to the complex behaviors of those who interact with it.

Part I. The Problem RMF Does Not Measure

Chapter 1. Why User Risk Exists

1. Introduction

Every major cybersecurity breach leaves behind a familiar conclusion: the controls were in place, yet the organization was still compromised. The explanation often points to human error, but that answer raises a more important question. If human decisions influence security outcomes so consistently, why are they rarely measured as part of organizational risk?

User Risk is the measurable likelihood that variability in human decision-making degrades system trust, control effectiveness, or mission assurance during operational use.

2. The Human Element as a Persistent Risk Source

The human element is often cited as the weakest link in security frameworks. A significant proportion of cybersecurity breaches are directly linked to human error, whether due to negligence, miscommunication, or a lack of awareness. Across industry and government reporting, compromised credentials, phishing, and user-driven errors consistently rank among the most common initial access vectors, reinforcing that human interaction remains a primary driver of cyber incidents [19], [9]. This evidence reinforces that User Risk is not a peripheral concern. It is a primary driver of cybersecurity outcomes.

The 2013 Target breach compromised approximately 40 million payment card records and 70 million customer records [51]. The attack originated through compromised credentials belonging to a third-party HVAC vendor, which attackers used to access Target's internal network. The incident shows how trusted external access, credential management, and vendor oversight can create organizational risk even when formal security controls exist.

3. Variability in Human Behavior

This variability manifests through situational factors such as workload, stress, and competing priorities. Under pressure, even skilled employees may overlook security procedures.

Research on decision-making under stress consistently shows that cognitive load, time pressure, and operational demands shift individuals toward faster, less deliberate choices, increasing the likelihood of security errors [56], [59]. For instance, an employee facing multiple deadlines may choose to bypass security protocols to expedite task completion. This variability highlights the necessity for organizations to develop security measures that accommodate human behavior rather than rely solely on compliance.

4. System Trust Versus Human Judgment

Control effectiveness ultimately depends on user interpretation and response. The Target data breach demonstrates how over-reliance on technical controls without behavioral accountability degrades operational security. Employees disregarded alerts indicating unauthorized access because they overrelied on technology rather than proactively engaging with security protocols [51]. This reliance illustrates how control measures can lead to complacency and highlights the need for a dual focus on both system efficacy and user understanding.

To address this gap, organizations should implement multi-layered security protocols that emphasize user involvement. Regular training and awareness programs can ensure employees understand the importance of their role in maintaining security, building an environment where proactive judgment is valued.

5. Evidence from Breach Data

Data consistently shows that User Risk is directly correlated with security incidents. Research confirms that human factors, including social engineering, errors, and misuse, play a dominant role in breach events. Incident response and threat intelligence reports show that social engineering, credential compromise, and user-initiated actions remain among the most common pathways to system intrusion, indicating that human behavior continues to be a primary driver of cyber incidents [3], [43], [44].

High-profile breaches, such as those experienced by Equifax and Yahoo, showcase that even advanced technological defenses can be undermined by inappropriate user actions.

In 2017, the Equifax breach was driven primarily by failure to remediate a known vulnerability in a timely manner and weaknesses in asset visibility that allowed vulnerable systems to remain exposed [14], [50]. The incident demonstrates how execution failures and unclear operational accountability can degrade security even when formal controls and governance structures exist.

The breach of Yahoo further illustrates how human decisions can amplify technical vulnerabilities. Between 2013 and 2014, attackers compromised billions of user accounts, in part through stolen credentials and forged authentication cookies that allowed persistent access without repeated login verification. Subsequent investigations revealed detection delays, incomplete internal communication, and insufficient user notification practices, all of which extended the breach's impact. These were not failures of technology alone.

They reflected breakdowns in user-driven processes such as credential management, monitoring, and incident response decision-making. The Yahoo incident demonstrates that when user actions and organizational responses lag behind threat activity, even large-scale platforms remain vulnerable [46].

6. The Role of Training and Policies

Organizations often assume that training and policy compliance reduce User Risk. In practice, course completion does not guarantee that users exercise correct judgment during operations.

Psychological factors, such as the tendency to disregard training once initial compliance is achieved, can hinder long-term behavioral change. To effectively combat this, organizations must develop engaging, ongoing training that emphasizes real-world scenarios.

7. Challenges in Measuring User Risk

Quantifying User Risk poses unique challenges. Unlike technical vulnerabilities, which can often be assessed through automated tools, User Risk is complex and qualitative. Existing risk assessment methodologies often emphasize compliance over a deeper understanding of behavior, leaving significant gaps.

To address these gaps, organizations can utilize:

- **Behavioral Analytics:** Implement tools that analyze User Risk patterns, identifying anomalies that could indicate security risk [17]. Until direct behavioral indicators are available, organizations approximate User Risk using methods such as behavioral analytics, simulations, and operational observations.
- **Scenario-Based Assessments:** Conduct regular scenario-based evaluations to measure how well employees respond to various security threats in

simulated environments.

- **Continuous Monitoring:** Employ continuous monitoring to observe user interactions with systems, thus gaining insights into compliance and potential risks.

8. Conclusion

User Risk is a vital yet often overlooked factor in cybersecurity risk assessments. Acknowledging the influence of human behavior enables organizations to develop a more comprehensive view of their security vulnerabilities and defenses.

As we progress through the subsequent chapters, we will explore how the RMF addresses User Risk, identify blind spots in authorization, and propose actionable solutions to measure and mitigate user-related vulnerabilities. This exploration aims to equip cybersecurity professionals and decision-makers with the tools necessary to integrate User Risk into their strategic frameworks, ultimately enhancing organizational resilience.

Closing Leadership Question

What evidence do you have that user decisions in your environment consistently preserve system trust during operations?

Chapter 2. How RMF Currently Treats Users

1. Introduction

Modern cybersecurity frameworks are remarkably effective at measuring technical safeguards. They document configurations, verify controls, and evaluate vulnerabilities with impressive precision. Yet the moment those frameworks encounter the people expected to operate those systems, the evidence becomes surprisingly thin.

Understanding how organizations approach User Risk is vital for developing improved strategies that integrate human factors into cybersecurity frameworks, ultimately building a more proactive security posture.

2. Traditional Risk Management Frameworks

Organizations commonly rely on established risk management frameworks to identify and mitigate risks. Prominent frameworks include:

NIST Cybersecurity Framework (CSF)

The NIST Cybersecurity Framework provides a structured approach to managing cybersecurity risk across five core functions: Identify, Protect, Detect, Respond, and Recover [34]. Version 2.0 expands this model by introducing a sixth function, Govern, which formalizes accountability and risk oversight. Despite this evolution, the framework still addresses User Risk primarily through policy enforcement and awareness activities rather than measurable behavioral risk scoring.

NIST Risk Management Framework (RMF)

The NIST Risk Management Framework, defined in Special Publication 800-37 Revision 2, establishes a seven-step process for categorizing systems, selecting and implementing controls, assessing effectiveness, authorizing operation, and continuously monitoring risk [31]. Authorization decisions rely on documented control implementations and assessment evidence. User behavior is addressed primarily through the Awareness and Training control family, where completion records serve as the dominant indicator of readiness. Demonstrated judgment under operational conditions is not required.

ISO/IEC 27001

The 2022 version of this standard for information security management systems focuses on establishing, implementing, maintaining, and improving an information security management system [26]. Clause 7 requires competence, awareness, and communication controls for personnel, but these requirements are satisfied through documentation and training records. The standard does not define how to score or compare User Risk as a risk variable.

Cybersecurity Maturity Model Certification (CMMC)

Developed by the U.S. Department of Defense and aligned with NIST SP 800-171, CMMC establishes tiered maturity levels for protecting Controlled Unclassified Information across the Defense Industrial Base [11]. The framework includes practices tied to awareness training and role-based access. Certification assessments confirm that practices exist and are documented. They do not evaluate whether users exercise security judgment correctly under real conditions.

Control Objectives for Information and Related Technologies (COBIT)

Published by ISACA, COBIT provides a governance and management framework for enterprise IT, emphasizing alignment between security and business objectives [22]. COBIT addresses human capital through people, skills, and competency components. These focus on organizational capability rather than individual behavioral risk.

Factor Analysis of Information Risk (FAIR)

FAIR is a quantitative risk model that decomposes risk into threat frequency, vulnerability, and probable loss magnitude [38]. It treats human actors as threat agents but models them primarily as sources of threat rather than as a measurable variable within the authorized workforce. Insider behavior is addressed as a threat scenario, not as a continuous governance input.

System and Organization Controls 2 (SOC 2)

SOC 2 evaluates service organizations against Trust Services Criteria covering security, availability, confidentiality, processing integrity, and privacy [1]. User controls appear under logical access and change management. Auditors confirm provisioning and revocation but do not assess how users interact with controls in practice.

While these frameworks provide strong governance and compliance structures, they share a limitation. Each addresses the user through process verification rather than behavioral measurement [6]. Policy existence is confirmed. Training delivery is tracked. Acknowledgment is recorded. None of these mechanisms produce evidence of how users perform when controls are stressed or when adversaries exploit human judgment. Traditional assessments prioritize technical vulnerabilities and documentation, leaving a measurable gap in how human factors inform authorization decisions [6].

3. The Limitations of Current Approaches

Overemphasis on Technology

Current risk management approaches often rely heavily on technology solutions. Organizations invest significantly in advanced security tools such as firewalls, intrusion detection systems, and endpoint protection, assuming these measures are sufficient. However, empirical evidence demonstrates that technology alone cannot mitigate user-driven risk. The Verizon Data Breach Investigations Report shows that the human element is involved in approximately 74% of breaches, including errors, privilege misuse, and social engineering [52]. This finding highlights a structural gap between technology-centric controls and the behavioral realities that drive security outcomes.

Compliance-Driven Mindset

Many organizations approach security from a compliance-driven perspective, focusing on meeting regulatory requirements rather than proactively addressing user-related vulnerabilities. This mentality can build complacency, as organizations may feel that achieving compliance equates to effective risk management.

For example, the General Data Protection Regulation establishes strict data protection requirements [13]. However, compliance alone does not ensure that users can recognize and respond to threats. Overreliance on compliance can lead to a false sense of security.

Lack of Continuous Monitoring

While organizations may implement user training initiatives periodically, these efforts often lack ongoing engagement or reinforcement. The SANS Institute reported that many organizations lack frequent refresher training, which contributes to declining awareness and retention over time [43].

Continuous monitoring of User Risk also remains underutilized in risk management, often overshadowed by more technical approaches. By not actively observing user interactions with systems, organizations miss critical opportunities to identify risky behaviors and intervene in a timely manner.

4. Evolving Approaches to User Risk Management

As the cybersecurity landscape continues to evolve, so too must the strategies employed to manage User Risk. Emerging approaches focus on integrating human factors into existing frameworks for more comprehensive risk management.

Behavior-Based Solutions

Behavior-based solutions use analytics and machine learning to identify patterns in User Risk. By analyzing how users interact with systems, organizations can detect anomalies that may indicate potential risks. For example, if most users access sensitive data during regular business hours, an unusual attempt to access that data at odd hours could trigger an alert.

Behavior-based analytics enables organizations to establish baselines of normal user activity and detect anomalies that may indicate elevated risk [17].

Gamified Training Programs

Recognizing the limitations of traditional training, organizations increasingly adopt gamified approaches to boost engagement and retention. These programs present security challenges in a competitive, interactive framework, which can resonate more effectively with users than standard training modules.

Gamified training approaches have been shown to increase user engagement and improve knowledge retention in cybersecurity learning environments [4].

For example, organizations can create security-themed competitions or simulations that place employees in scenarios where they must navigate potential threats.

Collaborative Security Culture

Developing a collaborative security culture builds greater responsibility among employees, transforming them from passive participants into active defenders of organizational security. Initiatives such as regular security briefings and feedback loops allow employees to share ideas and experiences, driving a sense of collective ownership of security within the organization.

Research indicates that organizations with mature incident response capabilities, visibility, and coordinated security processes experience improved breach outcomes and reduced impact [20]. Structured coordination, visibility, and response readiness consistently influence breach containment time and overall impact.

5. Challenges in Evolving User Risk Management

Despite the advancements in understanding and addressing User Risk, several challenges remain.

Resistance to Change

Changing organizational culture and practices often faces resistance. Employees might be accustomed to established procedures, making it difficult to implement new strategies or technologies.

Resource Constraints

Many organizations, particularly small and medium-sized enterprises, struggle with finite resources. Investing in emerging technologies or comprehensive training programs may not be feasible, limiting their ability to adapt to current User Risk threats.

Misalignment Between IT and Human Resources

A disconnect between IT security teams and Human Resources departments can hinder efforts to build a security-focused culture. Collaboration is essential to ensure employees receive the training and support they need to navigate an increasingly complex cybersecurity landscape.

6. Conclusion

The current approaches to managing User Risk are evolving but remain constrained by traditional mindsets that often prioritize technology over human factors. Recognizing these limitations is crucial for organizations striving to build a comprehensive risk management strategy that effectively integrates User Risk.

In the chapters ahead, we will explore solutions and frameworks designed to bridge the gap between technology and human behavior. Ultimately, this aims to create a more resilient cybersecurity posture across organizations. By recognizing User Risk as a critical element of overall cybersecurity, organizations can better prepare for the challenges that lie ahead.

Closing Leadership Question

Which user-related artifacts in your RMF package show how decisions are made during operations, not just how requirements were completed?

Chapter 3. The Authorization Blind Spot

1. Introduction

An Authorizing Official signs the authorization package. Months of engineering, assessment, documentation, and risk discussions culminate in a single decision. At that moment, the system is considered acceptable for operation.

Yet history shows that many significant breaches begin after that signature is applied.

2. Understanding Authorization and Its Limitations

Authorization decisions are predominantly driven by the quality and type of evidence presented during assessments. According to NIST, the RMF relies heavily on documentation demonstrating compliance with technical controls, including policies, configuration settings, system documentation, and vulnerability scanning results [31]. These artifacts provide evidence that safeguards exist and function as intended. They do not, however, provide equivalent evidence of how users will behave once the system enters routine operation.

RMF does not explicitly measure Behavioral Variability during operational use. As a result, RMF contains behavioral controls, such as awareness and training requirements, but lacks behavioral indicators that show how users actually exercise judgment in real environments.

This distinction is subtle but critical. Authorization decisions confirm that security mechanisms exist and function. They do not necessarily confirm how users will interpret, prioritize, or respond to those mechanisms once the system enters operational use.

Research in usable security reinforces the operational significance of this gap. Security mechanisms cannot be evaluated solely by their technical properties because their effectiveness also depends on how users understand and interact with them [60].

Authorization may establish that required safeguards exist and function as intended, but it cannot predict how consistently users will exercise judgment once those safeguards encounter real operational conditions.

A purely technical view of cybersecurity therefore leaves behavioral risk unaccounted for. Organizations may document control compliance, yet still remain exposed to risk created by human decisions under pressure, ambiguity, or incomplete context.

3. The Blind Spot in Risk Assessments

Evidence quality is central to effective risk assessments, particularly where User Risk is concerned. Technical controls generate concrete evidentiary artifacts. User-related evidence, by contrast, remains largely administrative and circumstantial. Training completion, policy acknowledgment, and procedural sign-off may all be documented, but those records do not verify whether users apply sound judgment under operational conditions.

This is the core blind spot. Organizations often assume that completed security activities translate into secure behavior. In practice, authorization artifacts show that requirements were satisfied, not that user decisions will preserve trust when operational pressure is high, or signals are ambiguous.

Control inheritance further compounds this issue. Enterprise-level controls may be assessed and accepted as effective, then inherited by downstream systems under the assumption that they will produce the same results everywhere. Yet inherited controls do not eliminate variability in how users respond. Differences in workload, authority, training quality, and mission tempo can significantly alter real-world outcomes.

Consider a hypothetical financial institution with strong enterprise authentication and transaction review processes. If a user is pressured to process transactions rapidly during peak workload, they may bypass or discount security checks to save time. The inherited control still exists. The operational outcome, however, now depends on human judgment rather than control design alone.

This gap matters because breach outcomes depend not only on whether controls exist, but on how they are used. Breach research shows that stronger detection, response maturity, and operational visibility reduce overall breach impact, reinforcing the need to incorporate Behavioral Evidence into risk decisions rather than infer it from compliance artifacts alone [20].

4. Clean ATOs and Fragile Trust

The phenomenon of clean ATOs existing alongside fragile Operational Trust relationships exemplifies the authorization blind spot. Systems can receive ATOs based on thorough documentation of controls without a comparable examination of how users will interact with those controls in practice. Trust in operational environments is therefore often presumed rather than tested.

Once a system receives an ATO, leadership tends to focus on compliance status, residual findings, and formal documentation. When breaches occur, they are frequently treated as isolated incidents rather than as symptoms of a structural weakness in how User Risk is represented in authorization decisions.

This disconnect is particularly dangerous because

technical validity can coexist with operational fragility. A system may remain fully compliant on paper while users make exception approvals, delay patching, mishandle privileged access, or misinterpret alerts in ways that erode control effectiveness over time.

The Equifax breach illustrates this problem clearly. Attackers exploited a known vulnerability in a public-facing application, but the broader organizational failure also reflected weaknesses in operational awareness, prioritization, and response. The controls framework existed. The trust relationship failed in practice.

5. Implicit User Risk Acceptance

The absence of User Risk assessment leads to implicit risk acceptance while allowing significant vulnerabilities to go unaddressed. Decision-makers may authorize systems based on presumed adherence to administrative controls, yet fail to consider how users actually act under real operational conditions. This results in risk narratives that are incomplete, inferred, and insufficiently examined at the leadership level.

As leaders rely on authorization decisions, it is essential to recognize that acceptance of user-related risk is often based on assumptions rather than direct Behavioral Evidence. This shifts the discussion of authorization away from simple procedural compliance and toward the need for a more complete model of how security decisions are made in practice.

Human Judgment must therefore be treated as a continuous factor in operational risk. Training still matters, but course completion alone does not show whether users will recognize suspicious activity, resist operational shortcuts, or preserve control intent under pressure.

6. Call to Action

Understanding the implications of the authorization blind spot requires a shift in how organizations frame and address risk. Leaders must evaluate not only whether controls are present, but also how user decisions influence those controls during routine operations. Continued reliance on ATOs without a comparable understanding of operational behavior creates an illusion of security that is not only misleading but potentially harmful.

This chapter therefore poses a central question: What assumptions about user judgment are embedded in your authorization decisions, and where are they explicitly evaluated? Organizations should begin developing methods that incorporate Behavioral Evidence into their risk management processes so that trust is assessed not only in architecture, but also in operation.

7. Discussion on Technology Interfaces

Technology interfaces play an important role in shaping User Risk related to security protocols. Interfaces that are overly complex, poorly designed, or burdensome can increase the likelihood of user error and encourage security workarounds. An overly complicated authentication flow, for example, may reduce adherence rather than improve it.

Technology, therefore, shapes behavior not only through enforcement but through usability.

For this reason, organizations should view user experience as part of their security architecture. Effective interfaces reduce friction, support timely decisions, and reinforce secure behavior without creating unnecessary operational burden. Security controls that are difficult to use may remain technically compliant while becoming behaviorally fragile.

8. Conclusion

The authorization blind spot represents a significant gap in how organizations assess and manage risk. By failing to incorporate User Risk into the risk assessment process, organizations create vulnerabilities that can degrade trust long after authorization is granted. The next chapter defines User Risk more precisely and establishes the conceptual foundation needed to measure and govern it.

Closing Leadership Question

What assumptions about user judgment are embedded in your authorization decisions, and where do you explicitly evaluate them?

Part II. Defining User Risk

Chapter 4. What User Risk Is and Is Not

1. Introduction

Ask ten cybersecurity professionals to define User Risk, and you are likely to receive ten different answers. Some equate it with insider threats. Others think of awareness training, policy violations, or simple user error. Those explanations describe pieces of the problem, but none define it completely.

RMF has matured around the ability to evaluate technical controls. Assessors verify configuration settings, analyze vulnerability data, and confirm that safeguards operate in accordance with policy.

RMF verifies that controls are implemented and operating as intended. What it does not explicitly measure is how human decision variability influences those controls during operational use.

This gap is central to understanding why User Risk remains difficult to evaluate within operational environments.

2. Defining User Risk

User Risk encompasses a broad range of behaviors, including intentional actions such as malicious insider activity and unintentional mistakes such as misconfigurations, delayed response, or failure to follow established protocols. It also includes risks associated with insufficient training, limited context, and behavior shaped by organizational culture.

Definition
User Risk: *User Risk is the measurable likelihood that human decision variability degrades system trust, control effectiveness, or mission assurance during operational use.*

A critical aspect of User Risk is its dynamic nature. It changes with turnover, mission tempo, organizational priorities, evolving technology, and shifts in authority or role. This dynamic quality is one reason User Risk is so difficult to assess through static documentation alone.

The financial consequences of this dynamic quality are measurable. Insider threat research shows that negligent User Risk accounts for approximately 56% of internal incidents and contributes to an average annual organizational cost exceeding $15 million [39].

3. What User Risk Is Not

User Risk is frequently misunderstood because it intersects with multiple established risk categories. Clarifying what User Risk is not is necessary to prevent overlap, misclassification, and ineffective mitigation strategies.

User Risk is not the same as insider threat. Insider threat focuses on malicious intent and adversarial behavior originating from within the organization. User Risk includes both malicious and non-malicious actions. It captures decision variability across the entire user population, including errors, misjudgments, and routine operational choices that degrade control effectiveness.

User Risk is not equivalent to technical vulnerability. Vulnerabilities exist within systems, configurations, and software. User Risk exists in how individuals interact with those systems. A vulnerability may be present, but exposure often depends on whether users recognize, prioritize, and act on it.

User Risk is not a measure of training completion. Training records demonstrate that information was delivered. They do not demonstrate that users apply that information under operational conditions. Completion metrics are administrative artifacts, not

Behavioral Evidence.

User Risk is not eliminated by policy. Policies define expected behavior and assign responsibility. They do not guarantee adherence. User Risk persists even in environments with well-documented and enforced policy frameworks because decisions are made under varying conditions, priorities, and pressures.

User Risk is not static. It cannot be fully captured through point-in-time assessments or documentation. It changes with personnel, workload, system complexity, and operational tempo. Static artifacts cannot represent dynamic decision-making.

User Risk is not solely a compliance issue. Compliance verifies that required controls, training, and documentation exist. It does not verify how users behave when controls are exercised during real-world operations.

Understanding these distinctions reinforces the central premise of this chapter. User Risk is a measurable, operational variable that reflects how human decision-making influences system trust after controls are implemented.

4. Principles of User Risk

User Risk emerges from the interaction between technical safeguards and human decision-making. While security frameworks focus primarily on control reliability, operational outcomes depend equally on how individuals interpret and apply those controls during system use. The following principles summarize the foundational characteristics of User Risk within operational cybersecurity environments.

Principle 1
Security controls do not eliminate human decision

variability.

Technical safeguards are designed to enforce requirements, but they frequently rely on users to interpret and execute operational actions. Access approvals, authentication prompts, configuration changes, and incident responses often require human judgment. Because individuals make decisions under varying conditions, the behavior associated with those actions introduces variability that cannot be fully eliminated through technical enforcement.

Multi-factor authentication is widely deployed to protect privileged access. However, the effectiveness of the control still depends on User Risk. If an employee approves an unexpected authentication request or repeatedly accepts prompts without verification, the control's protective value is reduced. The mechanism remains technically functional, but the outcome depends on the user's decision.

Principle 2
Authorization decisions validate system design, not operational behavior.

The authorization process evaluates whether security controls are properly implemented and operating as intended. Assessment artifacts such as configuration baselines, vulnerability scans, and policy documentation provide evidence that safeguards exist and function correctly. These evaluations establish confidence in the design and configuration of a system, but they rarely evaluate how users will interact with those safeguards during routine operation.

A system may receive an authorization to operate after demonstrating compliance with access control requirements, encryption standards, and monitoring policies. Once the system enters operational use, administrators may grant exceptions, approve elevated privileges, or delay security updates based on mission demands. These decisions influence the system's security posture even though the controls themselves remain compliant.

Principle 3

User Risk emerges after controls are implemented.

User Risk becomes operational after safeguards are implemented. Once systems enter daily use, Behavioral Variability begins to influence how those safeguards perform in practice.

A vulnerability management program may identify and prioritize remediation actions according to established policies. However, system administrators may delay patch deployment due to operational constraints or competing priorities. The vulnerability management process remains active, but the risk exposure increases because of Human Judgment regarding implementation timing.

Principle 4

Behavioral risk increases as system complexity increases.

Modern information systems integrate cloud services, automated orchestration, third-party platforms, and distributed administrative roles. As system complexity increases, the number of decisions required to manage and maintain those systems also increases. Each decision point introduces the potential for Behavioral Variability that can influence security outcomes.

In cloud environments, administrators frequently manage identity roles, network configurations, and storage permissions through management consoles or automated templates. A single misconfigured permission or incorrectly assigned role can expose sensitive data or administrative functions. The technical controls remain available, but the complexity of the decision environment increases the likelihood of error.

Principle 5

Unmeasured risk cannot be reliably governed.

Effective risk management depends on the ability to observe and evaluate the factors that influence security outcomes. Technical safeguards generate measurable indicators such as vulnerability counts, configuration compliance scores, and monitoring alerts. Human Judgment rarely produces equivalent metrics, which limits an organization's ability to assess behavioral influence on operational security.

Security awareness training programs often track completion rates as evidence of compliance. While completion records demonstrate participation, they do not reveal whether individuals recognize malicious activity, respond appropriately to security alerts, or apply secure practices during operational tasks. Without behavioral indicators, organizations must rely on assumption rather than measurable evidence when evaluating User Risk.

5. The Impact of User Behavior on Security Posture

User behavior directly influences organizational security posture and must be treated as a risk factor in its own right. Breach reporting consistently shows that misuse, error, credential abuse, and social engineering remain central drivers of incident outcomes [52].

The Equifax breach provides a useful example. The failure to remediate a known vulnerability exposed sensitive data belonging to nearly 147 million individuals. While the technical weakness was specific, the broader failure reflected problems in decision-making, prioritization, and organizational execution that allowed the vulnerability to persist.

Everyday convenience decisions can also introduce security exposure when they bypass established controls. This is why User Risk must be treated as an operational factor rather than an assumed byproduct of completed training or signed policy acknowledgments.

6. Assessing User Risk

To integrate User Risk into existing frameworks, organizations must establish practical methods for assessing it. This involves identifying observable indicators and developing a more complete understanding of how users behave in operational environments.

No single methodology captures User Risk completely. Organizations that successfully integrate behavioral evidence typically combine several complementary approaches. Some improve visibility into user behavior, while others strengthen governance or provide leaders with better evidence for authorization decisions. Together, they create a more complete understanding of Operational Trust.

A risk-based approach can include:

- **User Behavior Analytics (UBA):** Monitoring user activity patterns can provide insight into anomalies that may indicate security risk, such as unusual access requests, unexpected login behavior, or repeated policy overrides. Behavioral analytics enables the detection of anomalous activity by establishing baselines of normal User Risk and identifying deviations in real time [17].
- **Phishing Simulations:** Regular simulation exercises can help organizations evaluate how users respond to deceptive communications and how susceptibility changes over time. Organizations that implement continuous phishing awareness and simulation

programs improve their ability to recognize and respond to social engineering attempts over time [40].

- **Training and Awareness Programs:** Training remains an important mitigation mechanism, but its value should be assessed through observable behavior, not completion metrics alone.

7. Addressing Organizational Culture

Organizational culture is a pivotal factor influencing User Risk and organizational security. A culture that prioritizes security can improve compliance, encourage reporting, and reinforce thoughtful decision-making. A culture that treats security as an administrative burden can normalize shortcuts, silence concerns, and reward speed over sound judgment.

Leadership plays a critical role in shaping security culture. When executives discuss cybersecurity openly, model responsible behavior, and reinforce the importance of secure decision-making, they influence how users interpret security expectations. Regular communication, visible support for secure practices, and open dialogue about threats create an environment in which users feel responsible for maintaining trust.

Organizations that invest in coordination, visibility, and response maturity generally experience better breach outcomes and lower overall impact than those with fragmented or siloed security practices [20].

8. Operational Mitigation Measures

To mitigate User Risk effectively, organizations can adopt several approaches:

- **Conduct Regular Security Awareness Training:** Implement continuous programs using realistic scenarios, timely updates, and role-specific examples.
- **Create Clear and Accessible Security Policies:**

Ensure policies are understandable, usable, and easy to find so that users can apply them under operational pressure.

- **Encourage Reporting of Incidents:** Establish a non-punitive reporting environment so users can raise concerns quickly without fear of reprisal.
- **Leverage Technology Solutions:** Use behavioral analytics, multi-factor authentication, and automated alerts to add visibility and reinforce secure actions.

Measurement Versus Mitigation

User Risk measurement and User Risk mitigation are distinct activities.

Training programs, awareness campaigns, and policy education attempt to influence behavior. These activities mitigate risk, but they do not measure whether human judgment actually improves during operational decision-making.

Measurement answers a different question. It examines how users make decisions after controls and training already exist. Without measurement, organizations cannot determine whether mitigation strategies meaningfully change risk outcomes.

9. Operational Scenario

Consider a retail organization during a high-volume sales period. A point-of-sale operator receives repeated automated alerts flagging unusual transaction patterns consistent with stolen payment credentials. Under workload pressure, the operator dismisses the alerts without investigation, assuming the system's fraud detection controls will escalate or block any genuine threat independently.

The system had correctly identified a pattern associated with compromised cards. No escalation occurred because the control depended on user acknowledgment to trigger the next step. The operator's decision to defer the alerts effectively disabled that control during the period of highest exposure.

Financial losses and reputational damage followed before the pattern was identified through end-of-day reconciliation.

RMF Control Gap

IR, Incident Response

Automated alerting functioned as designed

Gap: RMF evaluates whether incident response procedures exist and are documented, not whether users act on alerts effectively under operational pressure

SI, System and Information Integrity

Fraud detection controls were active and generating valid signals

Gap: RMF verifies that monitoring tools are implemented, not that user decisions preserve the integrity of detection workflows during high-tempo operations

AT, Awareness and Training

Training requirements were satisfied

Gap: RMF tracks completion, not whether users apply sound judgment when automated controls require human confirmation to function

Operational Insight

The control did not fail technically. It failed at the decision point. The system produced the correct signal. The user's response determined the outcome. This is the gap RMF authorization evidence does not capture:

not whether the alert fired, but whether the person who received it acted on it.

10. Conclusion

Defining User Risk is essential for comprehensive organizational risk management. By recognizing the dynamic nature of User Risk, assessing its operational impact, and distinguishing mitigation from measurement, organizations can build a more complete view of security. Future chapters will explore how User Risk can be integrated into authorization and governance processes to address the blind spots identified in earlier discussions.

Closing Leadership Question

What evidence shows that authorized user actions in your environment consistently preserve system trust?

Chapter 5. User Risk as a Trust Variable

1. Introduction

Trust is often treated as a byproduct of successful control implementation. In reality, trust is earned every day through the interaction between technical safeguards and Human Judgment.

2. The Importance of Integrating User Risk

Integrating User Risk into cybersecurity frameworks is essential because user actions directly influence the effectiveness of technical controls. Organizations that fail to account for human behavior leave their security posture incomplete. Breach research shows that improved visibility, response maturity, and security automation are associated with materially lower breach costs and faster containment [20].

User errors, both unintentional and intentional, represent a substantial portion of security incidents. Organizations that combine awareness programs, phishing simulations, and usable security controls are better positioned to reduce user susceptibility to social engineering over time [40].

3. The Operational Trust Model

Security frameworks exist to establish confidence that systems will operate securely. This confidence is typically derived from the implementation and assessment of technical safeguards. Controls are cataloged, implemented, and verified through structured assessment processes. When these safeguards function as intended, systems are considered trustworthy from a technical perspective.

However, Operational Trust in a system does not depend solely on the reliability of its controls. It also depends on how users interact with those controls during operational use. Security mechanisms frequently require human decisions. Users approve authentication requests, configure access permissions, manage administrative accounts, and respond to operational alerts. Each of these actions introduces an element of human judgment into the system's functioning.

Definition
Operational Trust = Control Reliability × Human Judgment

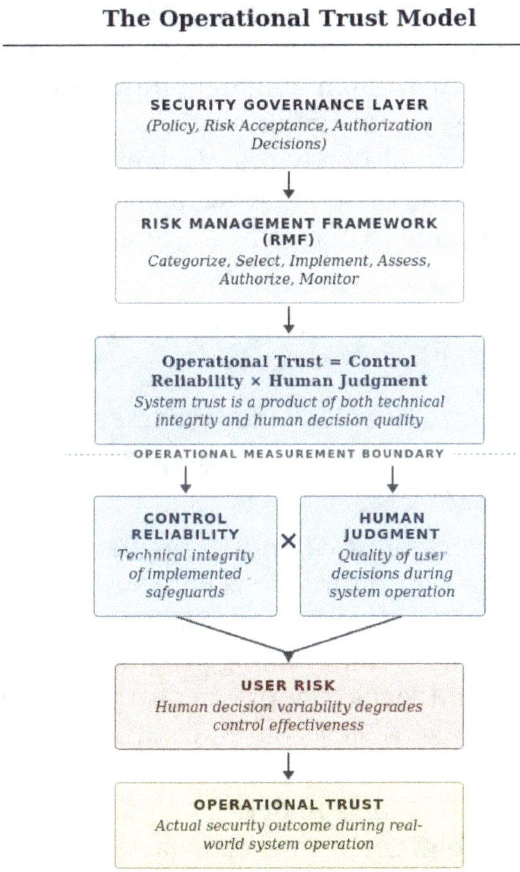

Figure 1. Operational Trust Model

Figure 1 illustrates how Operational Trust emerges

from the interaction between Control Reliability and Human Judgment. Reliable technical safeguards establish the foundation for secure operation, but they do not determine operational outcomes by themselves. Every authentication approval, privilege assignment, configuration change, exception request, and incident response introduces Human Judgment into the operation of the system.

RMF rigorously evaluates Control Reliability through technical assessments, configuration validation, and continuous monitoring. What it does not explicitly measure is how Human Judgment influences those controls once systems enter routine operation. User Risk describes that Behavioral Variability. Operational Trust reflects the resulting level of confidence that controls continue to perform as intended in the real world.

4. Methodologies for Integrating User Risk Assessments

To integrate User Risk into cybersecurity frameworks effectively, organizations can adopt several methodologies:

- **Risk Assessments:** Conduct regular assessments that evaluate user interactions with systems. These assessments can identify at-risk behaviors and provide insights for improving training programs. Surveys, interviews, and focus groups can also yield useful qualitative data.
- **Behavior Analytics:** Use user and entity behavior analytics (UEBA) tools to detect anomalous activity and establish baselines for normal behavior. This helps identify potentially malicious activity or compromised accounts more quickly.
- **Continuous Feedback Loops:** Establish mechanisms for continuous feedback about User Risk.

Post-incident reviews, after-action assessments, and decision-point analysis can inform future training and governance improvements.

5. Building Organizational Support for User Risk Integration

Successfully integrating User Risk is not solely a technical effort. It requires visible organizational support, executive sponsorship, and a culture that values secure decision-making as much as technical excellence. The following practices help create that environment.

- **Leadership Commitment:** Executive support is essential for cultivating a culture where security is prioritized. Leaders should model security-conscious behavior and actively reinforce expectations.
- **Open Communication:** Encouraging users to report vulnerabilities, suspicious activity, or mistakes without fear of undue punishment improves visibility and strengthens accountability.
- **Regular Training:** Consistent, varied training opportunities help keep security expectations current and visible.
- **Gamified Training Platforms:** Interactive tools, simulations, and quizzes can increase engagement and improve retention.
- **Employee Recognition Programs:** Recognizing individuals or teams who model sound security behavior can reinforce positive norms.

6. Measuring the Effectiveness of User Risk Integration

Once User Risk has been integrated into cybersecurity frameworks, organizations must measure its effectiveness to support continuous improvement. Key performance indicators can include:

- **Incident Response Times:** Faster response often indicates better awareness, stronger coordination, and more effective operational judgment.
- **Phishing Simulation Results:** Repeated improvements in recognizing and reporting phishing attempts can provide useful insight into susceptibility trends.
- **User Engagement Metrics:** Training participation, feedback quality, and reporting behavior can help assess whether awareness efforts are being internalized.

7. Case Study: Integrating User Risk into Cybersecurity Practice, Lessons from the Capital One Data Breach

The 2019 Capital One breach exposed the personal data of approximately 106 million individuals in the United States and Canada. The attacker, a former cloud service employee, exploited a misconfigured web application firewall to gain access to cloud storage resources [47].

While the initial vulnerability was technical, the breach escalated due to user-driven factors. The attacker used excessive permissions and accessed sensitive data using valid credentials and authorized pathways. Data exfiltration occurred over an extended period before detection.

In 2020, U.S. regulators fined Capital One $80 million, citing failure to establish effective risk assessment processes and inadequate controls around access and configuration management [37].

RMF Control Mapping and User Risk Exposure

AC, Access Control

- Overly permissive roles allowed broad access to sensitive data

- Gap: RMF validates role definitions, not how users or administrators over-provision access in practice

IA, Identification and Authentication

- Access occurred through valid authentication mechanisms
- Gap: RMF confirms identity enforcement, not misuse of legitimate credentials

CM, Configuration Management

- Misconfigured firewall enabled initial access
- Gap: RMF assesses configuration baselines, not continuous user-driven configuration drift

AU, Audit and Accountability

- Logging existed but did not trigger timely detection
- Gap: RMF confirms audit capability, not the effectiveness of monitoring user-driven anomalies

IR, Incident Response

- Breach was discovered externally, not through internal detection
- Gap: RMF evaluates response plans, not whether User Risk triggers detection

AT, Awareness and Training

- Administrative and operational decisions contributed to misconfiguration and over-permissioning
- Gap: RMF tracks training completion, not the quality of user decision-making in configuration and access management

Post-Breach Integration of User Risk

Following the breach, Capital One implemented changes that directly integrated User Risk into cybersecurity operations:

- Reduced excessive permissions through stricter identity and access governance
- Enhanced cloud configuration monitoring and automated compliance checks
- Expanded logging and real-time alerting tied to user activity in cloud environments
- Strengthened security training for developers and cloud engineers focused on secure configuration practices
- Increased investment in behavioral analytics to detect anomalous access patterns

Measurable Outcomes

- Improved visibility into user activity within cloud environments
- Reduced risk of privilege misuse through tighter access controls
- Faster detection of anomalous behavior through enhanced monitoring

Regulatory findings confirmed that post-breach remediation focused heavily on improving governance over user access and configuration decisions, not just technical controls.

What RMF Would Have Reported Pre-Breach

- Access controls implemented
- Authentication mechanisms in place
- Configuration baselines defined
- Logging enabled
- Incident response plans documented
- Training completed
- System likely maintained an Authorization to Operate.

What Was Missing

- Measurement of privilege escalation risk

- Continuous validation of configuration decisions by users
- Behavioral monitoring of access patterns
- Detection of abnormal but authorized activity

Operational Insight

The breach did not occur because controls were absent. It occurred because user decisions, configuration choices, and permission models degraded control effectiveness.

Capital One's response focused on integrating User Risk into security oversight:

- Access decisions became continuously evaluated
- Configuration actions became monitored events
- User activity became a primary detection signal

This case reinforces a central principle:

Security controls define structure. User behavior defines exposure.

8. Conclusion

Integrating User Risk assessments into cybersecurity frameworks is essential for strengthening security posture. By adopting methodologies that recognize the importance of User Risk, leveraging technology, and building a culture of security awareness, organizations can reduce behavioral exposure and improve resilience. The next chapter turns to training as a mitigation strategy and clarifies how it differs from measurement.

Closing Leadership Question

What indicators do you review to determine whether trust in your systems is strengthening or eroding during normal operations?

Chapter 6. Training as a Mitigation Strategy

1. Introduction

Organizations spend billions of dollars each year teaching people how to recognize cyber threats. Yet successful phishing attacks, credential theft, and preventable errors continue to dominate breach statistics. The problem is not that training lacks value. The problem is that training and measurement answer different questions.

Training teaches users what to do. Measurement reveals what they actually do [42].

This chapter examines how training functions as a mitigation strategy, what effective programs entail, and how organizations can assess its impact without conflating training with measurement.

2. Key Elements of Successful Training Programs

Successful training and awareness programs should include several core elements if they are to influence behavior meaningfully.

- **Relevance:** Training should be tailored to the organization's operational context, threat profile, and user roles. Topics such as phishing, password management, privileged access, and data handling should be prioritized according to real risk exposure.
- **Engagement:** Programs should require active participation rather than passive completion. Quizzes, simulations, short scenario drills, and decision-based exercises help users apply concepts rather than merely acknowledge them.
- **Accessibility:** Training resources should be available in formats that accommodate different locations, schedules, and work patterns. Flexible delivery improves participation and increases the likelihood that security guidance will be used when

needed.

- **Ongoing Learning:** Threats evolve continuously, so training cannot be treated as a single annual event. Regular refreshers, timely updates, and reinforcement through scenario-based communication are necessary to keep security expectations active.

3. Effective Training Methods

Organizations can use multiple training methods to improve understanding and reduce susceptibility to common attack techniques.

- **E-Learning Modules:** Online modules allow users to complete foundational instruction at their own pace and can be adapted to different job functions.
- **Phishing Simulations:** Repeated simulation exercises help organizations evaluate how users respond to deceptive communications and whether reporting behavior improves over time. Proofpoint's 2023 State of the Phish report shows that simulated phishing reporting rates increased to 17%, while failure rates remained at 10%, illustrating the value of ongoing measurement rather than one-time awareness events [40].
- **Workshops and Seminars:** Live sessions allow users to discuss real scenarios, ask questions, and interpret security expectations in context. This is especially useful for high-risk roles that make frequent judgment calls.
- **Microlearning:** Short, focused updates can reinforce a single concept quickly and are easier to absorb during normal work routines than long, infrequent training events.

4. Building a Culture of Cybersecurity Awareness

Creating a culture of cybersecurity awareness requires leadership commitment and consistent reinforcement across the organization.

- **Leadership Involvement:** When executives participate in training and discuss security as an operational priority, they reinforce that secure behavior is expected at every level.
- **Encouraging Open Dialogue:** Users should be able to report suspicious activity, uncertainty, or mistakes without fear of disproportionate punishment. Open communication improves reporting quality and increases visibility into behavioral risk.
- **Recognition and Incentives:** Recognition can reinforce the value of secure behavior when it rewards reporting, verification, and careful decision-making rather than mere task completion.
- **Regular Communication:** Security reminders, timely updates, and discussion of recent incidents help maintain awareness and keep decision criteria visible in daily work.

5. Measuring Training Program Effectiveness

Measuring a training program requires looking beyond attendance records. Organizations need evidence that training changes operational behavior rather than simply satisfying administrative requirements. The following measures provide different perspectives on effectiveness.

- **Completion Rates:** Completion data can show whether training was delivered, but it does not by itself demonstrate improved judgment.
- **Feedback and Assessment Scores:** Knowledge checks can show whether users understood the material presented.
- **Incident Trend Review:** Changes in reporting behavior, phishing susceptibility, repeated policy violations, and escalation quality can provide more meaningful indicators of whether training is influencing

operational decisions.

- **Phishing Simulation Results:** Simulation performance can reveal whether users recognize suspicious content, report it appropriately, or still act on malicious prompts.

The key distinction is that training metrics measure exposure to content, while User Risk measurement examines how people behave after that content has already been delivered.

6. Case Study: Training Effectiveness and Behavioral Change, Lessons from Google Phishing Defense Program

To illustrate the measurable impact of training and awareness on User Risk, consider Google's internal anti-phishing initiative following repeated credential-targeting attacks against its workforce.

Google conducted a large-scale study of employee susceptibility to phishing and found that even highly technical users were vulnerable to credential harvesting. Initial phishing simulation campaigns demonstrated measurable click and credential submission rates across the organization, confirming that training completion alone did not equate to secure behavior [16].

In response, Google implemented a behavior-focused security program aligned with operational risk:

- Mandatory phishing simulations across the enterprise
- Immediate feedback loops for users who interacted with malicious emails
- Targeted retraining for high-risk users based on observed behavior
- Deployment of hardware-based multi-factor authentication keys for high-value accounts

- Continuous measurement of user interaction with simulated attacks

Measurable Outcomes

- Google reported a near-elimination of successful phishing attacks against employees who used hardware security keys. Internal testing showed:

- 0% successful account takeovers via phishing for users with security keys
- Significant reduction in credential submission rates across repeated simulations
- Increased reporting rates of suspicious emails over time

These results were later validated in public reporting, demonstrating that combining training with enforced authentication controls materially reduced user-driven risk [15].

RMF Control Mapping and Behavioral Impact

AT, Awareness and Training

- Training shifted from completion-based to behavior-measured
- Phishing simulations provided direct evidence of user decision-making
- Gap addressed: RMF tracks training completion, not effectiveness

IA, Identification and Authentication

- Hardware security keys strengthened authentication assurance
- Eliminated reliance on passwords vulnerable to phishing
- Gap addressed: RMF verifies MFA presence, not resistance to real-world attacks

AU, Audit and Accountability

- User interactions with phishing simulations were logged and analyzed
- Behavioral trends tracked over time
- Gap addressed: RMF confirms logging, not behavioral pattern analysis

IR, Incident Response

- Increased user reporting improved detection speed
- Reduced dwell time for phishing campaigns
- Gap addressed: RMF evaluates response plans, not user-triggered detection

What RMF Would Have Reported Pre-Program

- Training requirements satisfied
- Authentication controls implemented
- Logging enabled
- Incident response procedures documented

What Was Missing

- Measured phishing susceptibility
- Real-time behavioral response to simulated threats
- Correlation between training and user decision outcomes

Operational Insight

The result was not improved compliance. It was reduced exploitability.

- Google's program did not assume that training alone reduces risk. It treated User Risk as a measurable variable:
- Users were tested under realistic conditions
- Outcomes were tracked and used to adjust controls
- Authentication controls were strengthened based on observed failure modes

This case reinforces a key principle:

- Training completion demonstrates exposure to

information. User behavior demonstrates whether that information changes risk.

7. Conclusion

Training improves knowledge. Measurement evaluates judgment under operational conditions [42]. Security programs require both. Effective training can reduce exposure, but it does not by itself reveal whether user decision-making improves under operational conditions. The next chapter turns to policy integration and explains how organizations can translate behavioral expectations into governance structures.

Closing Leadership Question

How do you ensure your training programs improve User Risk, not just deliver information?

Part III. Measuring What RMF Cannot See

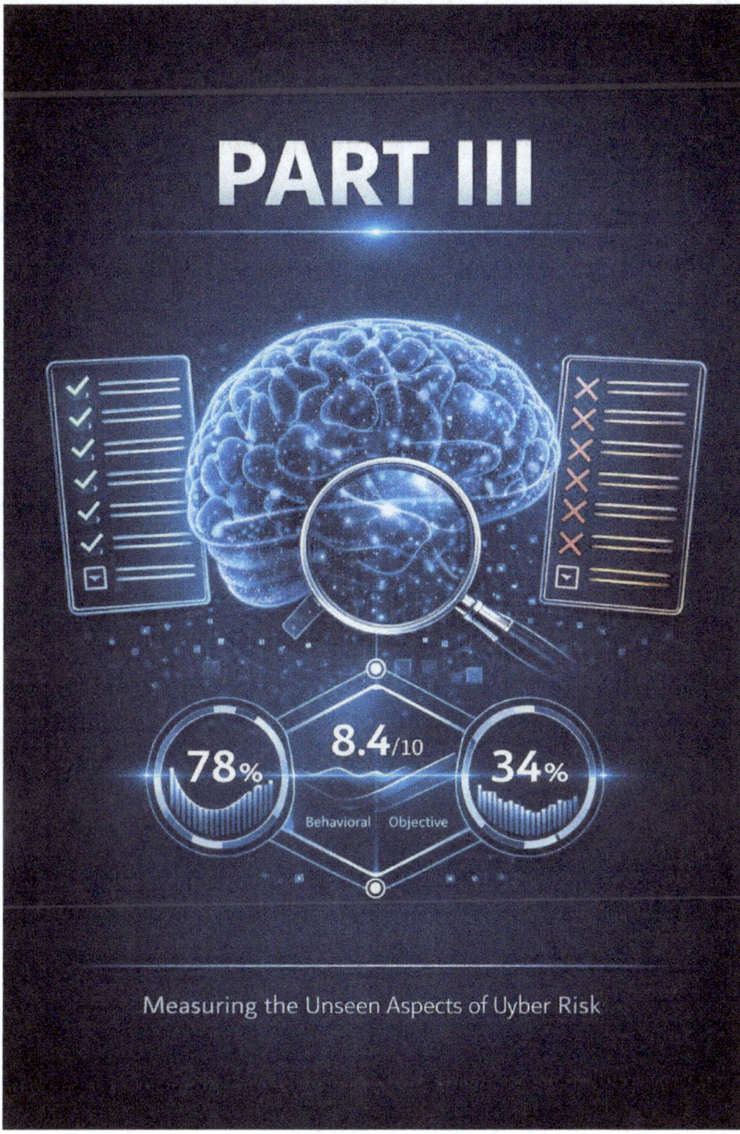

Chapter 7. Policies as Evidence Sources

1. Introduction

Every organization has security policies. Very few know whether those policies actually change behavior.

Policies translate what organizations learn about User Risk into enforceable expectations. If training shapes awareness and measurement reveals decision quality, policy defines how those decisions are governed during operations.

Most security policies describe what users are expected to do. Fewer reflect how users actually behave under operational conditions. This gap limits their effectiveness. When policies are disconnected from real decision patterns, they become administrative artifacts rather than operational controls.

Integrating User Risk into policy requires a shift in perspective. Policies must be informed by observed behavior, not assumed compliance. They should define expectations at the points where user decisions influence system trust, including access approval, exception handling, reporting, and escalation.

This chapter examines how organizations can align policy with observed User Risk, reinforce accountability, and use policy as a mechanism to govern decision-making in operational environments.

2. The Role of Policies in Managing User Risk

Policies informed by User Risk assessments can guide organizations in implementing preventive measures, establishing clear expectations, and building accountability, but they do not guarantee behavioral compliance [2]. They define expected conduct, assign responsibility, and establish the procedures users are expected to follow.

An effective cybersecurity policy framework should explicitly acknowledge User Risk. Policies that account for behavioral patterns can help reduce vulnerabilities stemming from human error, routine workarounds, and intentional misuse. Policy should therefore do more than declare requirements. It should reflect how decisions are actually made in operational environments.

3. Strategies for Incorporating User Risk into Policies

Policies influence behavior only when they reflect operational reality. Organizations seeking to reduce User Risk should design policy around the decisions users actually make rather than the idealized behaviors policy assumes.

- **Risk-Based Policy Development:** Develop policies based on the User Risks most likely to influence security outcomes. Tailor requirements to the decision points where users create, preserve, or degrade trust.
- **Establish Clear Roles and Responsibilities:** Define which users are responsible for approvals, reporting, exception handling, and escalation. Clarity improves accountability.
- **Integrate User Feedback:** Incorporating user feedback during policy development helps ensure that policies are relevant, realistic, and supportive of reporting behaviors that improve organizational security awareness [2].
- **Promote Flexibility and Adaptability:** Cyber threats evolve rapidly, so policies must be reviewed and updated regularly to reflect changing workflows, technologies, and threat conditions.

4. Best Practices for Policy Implementation

The effective implementation of policy requires

practices that support comprehension and compliance.

- **Communication and Awareness:** Policies should be reinforced through training, internal messaging, and scenario-based discussion.
- **User-Friendly Documentation:** Policies written in overly legalistic or technical language are less likely to shape actual behavior. Clear language improves operational usability.
- **Regular Training and Reinforcement:** Policy education should be tied to recurring exercises and real examples so that users understand how policy applies during daily work.
- **Monitoring and Accountability:** Organizations should review policy adherence through audits, observed behavior, exception patterns, and incident trends rather than relying solely on acknowledgment records.

5. Aligning Policies with Organizational Culture

For policies to be effective, they must align with organizational culture.

- **Leadership Commitment:** Leaders must model compliance and reinforce the importance of secure decision-making.
- **Encouraging a Non-Punitive Environment:** Users should be able to raise concerns, report mistakes, and seek clarification without fear of disproportionate punishment. This openness improves reporting behavior and provides more accurate insight into policy effectiveness and areas for improvement [2].
- **Celebrating Successes:** Recognizing secure behavior helps reinforce the idea that policy is an operational asset, not merely an administrative requirement.

6. Continuous Improvement and Evaluation

Integrating User Risk into policy is not a one-time effort. It requires continuous review and refinement.

- **Performance Metrics:** Track metrics such as incident reporting speed, exception frequency, repeated violations, and policy comprehension feedback. Establishing performance metrics can help measure the effectiveness of policies and identify gaps between expected and actual User Risk [2].
- **Regular Policy Reviews:** Schedule periodic reviews to ensure policies remain relevant and usable under current conditions.
- **Engaging External Expertise:** Independent review can help identify where policy language, implementation, or measurement remain disconnected from actual User Risk.

7. Case Study: Policy Integration and User Risk, Lessons from the Wells Fargo Account Fraud Scandal

Wells Fargo faced a large-scale internal misconduct incident in which employees created approximately 3.5 million unauthorized customer accounts over several years. While not a traditional cyber breach, the case reflects a systemic failure of policy design, User Risk alignment, and governance enforcement.

Investigations found that employees operated within established systems and access controls but made decisions driven by misaligned incentives, unclear expectations for escalation, and cultural pressure. Policies existed, but they did not reflect how users actually behaved under operational conditions.

Regulatory actions resulted in over $3 billion in penalties from multiple agencies, including the Consumer Financial Protection Bureau and the Office of the Comptroller of the Currency [57].

RMF Control Mapping and Policy Breakdown

PL, Planning (Policy and Procedures)

- Policies were documented but misaligned with operational behavior
- Gap: RMF validates policy existence, not alignment with real-world user incentives and actions

AT, Awareness and Training

- Employees were trained on procedures
- Gap: RMF tracks training completion, not whether users follow policy under pressure

IA, Identification and Authentication

- Users operated with valid credentials
- Gap: RMF confirms identity controls, not misuse of authorized access

AC, Access Control

- Systems allowed account creation within user roles
- Gap: RMF validates permissions, not abuse of legitimate functions

AU, Audit and Accountability

- Activities were logged but not escalated effectively
- Gap: RMF confirms logging, not enforcement of accountability tied to User Risk

IR, Incident Response

- Misconduct persisted over time before enterprise-level action
- Gap: RMF evaluates response structure, not responsiveness to policy violations

Policy Integration and Organizational Response

Following the scandal, Wells Fargo implemented structural reforms focused on aligning policy with User

Risk:

- Rewrote sales and account management policies to remove incentive-driven misconduct
- Strengthened internal reporting and escalation procedures for employees
- Expanded monitoring of employee activity tied to customer account actions
- Increased leadership accountability for policy enforcement
- Implemented cultural and training reforms emphasizing ethical decision-making

Measurable Outcomes

- Elimination of sales quotas tied to account creation
- Increased internal reporting of policy violations
- Enhanced oversight of user activity linked to customer data and accounts

Regulatory reviews confirmed that remediation focused on governance, accountability, and behavioral alignment, not just technical control changes.

What RMF Would Have Reported Pre-Incident

- Policies documented and approved
- Training completed
- Access controls enforced
- Logging enabled
- Oversight structures defined

What Was Missing

- Alignment between policy and user incentives
- Measurement of policy adherence in practice
- Detection of abnormal but authorized user activity
- Accountability mechanisms tied to behavior, not documentation

Operational Insight

The incident did not result from the absence of policy. It resulted from policy that did not reflect how users operated in real-world conditions. The corrective actions did not eliminate User Risk. They aligned governance with observed behavior:

- Policies were rewritten to reflect operational reality
- User actions became subject to continuous oversight
- Reporting and escalation became normalized behaviors

This case reinforces a key principle:

- Policy defines expected behavior. User actions define actual risk.

8. Conclusion

Integrating User Risk into policy is essential for managing user-related vulnerabilities and aligning governance with observed User Risk [2]. Policies that reflect real User Risk, accountability, and continuous improvement strengthen security governance. The next chapter turns to technology and examines how technical tools can support visibility into behavioral risk without replacing Human Judgment.

Closing Leadership Question

How do your policies reflect how users actually make decisions during operations, not just how they are expected to behave?

Chapter 8. Leveraging Technology Solutions

1. Introduction

Technology has given cybersecurity unprecedented visibility into systems. Ironically, it has also exposed one of its greatest blind spots. Organizations can monitor almost every aspect of a network in real time, yet still struggle to explain how human decisions influence security outcomes.

This chapter examines technological solutions that support User Risk management, explores their applications, and discusses best practices for implementation.

2. Technology Solutions for Identifying User Risk

Several technologies can help organizations identify user-related risk signals.

- **User and Entity Behavior Analytics (UEBA):** UEBA solutions analyze patterns of user activity to establish a behavioral baseline. Using machine learning algorithms, these tools detect anomalies that may indicate elevated risk, such as unusual login locations, excessive data access, or the use of unauthorized applications [17].
- **Security Information and Event Management (SIEM):** SIEM platforms aggregate and analyze log data from multiple sources within an organization. By correlating events and user activity, SIEMs can identify patterns indicative of insider threats and support continuous monitoring and response to security incidents [3].
- **Data Loss Prevention (DLP):** DLP solutions monitor and control the transfer of sensitive information, helping to prevent data breaches caused by user mistakes or malicious intent. These tools can enforce policies related to data handling and access, reducing the likelihood of data exposure due to user

error or misuse.

These tools do not measure intent directly. They help organizations observe patterns that may indicate elevated risk and support earlier intervention.

Identifying User Risk is only the first step. Once behavioral patterns become visible, organizations must determine how technology can reduce exposure without replacing Human Judgment.

3. Technology Solutions for Risk Mitigation

Once User Risks are identified, organizations can use technology to reduce exposure.

- **Multi-Factor Authentication (MFA):** Implementing MFA enhances account security by requiring users to provide multiple forms of verification before accessing systems or sensitive data. This added layer of protection reduces the risk of unauthorized access resulting from compromised credentials [32].
- **Endpoint Detection and Response (EDR):** EDR solutions monitor endpoint devices for suspicious activities and potential threats. EDR tools enhance visibility into endpoint activity and support detection and response to user-originated security risks.
- **Security Awareness Training Tools:** Technology can also enhance training initiatives. Various platforms offer gamified learning experiences, interactive simulations, and quizzes to engage employees in cybersecurity awareness training. By leveraging technology for training, organizations can improve engagement and knowledge retention among users [4].

4. Best Practices for Implementing Technology Solutions

To maximize the effectiveness of technology solutions for User Risk management, organizations should follow several best practices.

- **Conduct a Thorough Needs Assessment:** Before implementing any technology solution, organizations should conduct a comprehensive needs assessment to identify specific security challenges and User Risk areas. Understanding the organization's unique context will guide the selection of appropriate tools.
- **Involve Relevant Stakeholders:** Engaging stakeholders from various departments, such as IT, HR, compliance, and legal, during the selection and implementation of technology solutions ensures that a holistic approach is taken. Collaboration can lead to more effective solutions tailored to organizational needs.
- **Establish Clear Policies and Configurations:** When implementing new technology, organizations should ensure that policies align with the capabilities of the technology. Clear guidelines and configurations can help ensure that the technology is used effectively and in line with organizational security objectives.
- **Regularly Update and Improve Technologies:** Cyber threats evolve continually, making it essential for organizations to regularly update and improve their technology solutions. Continuous monitoring and adaptation are critical to maintaining a robust security posture.

5. Measuring the Effectiveness of Technology Solutions

Organizations should evaluate the effectiveness of their technology solutions through meaningful operational metrics.

- **Incident Reduction Rates:** Monitoring the frequency of security incidents before and after implementing technology solutions provides insight into their effectiveness. A reduction in incidents over time may indicate improved risk management effectiveness when evaluated alongside detection and response metrics [20].

- **User Adoption Rates:** Tracking user engagement and adoption of security technologies (such as MFA or DLP) can provide insights into the effectiveness of education and training initiatives.
- **Response Times:** Evaluating the time taken to detect and respond to security incidents can help organizations determine the responsiveness of their technology solutions. Faster detection and response times are associated with reduced breach impact and improved incident outcomes [20].

IBM Security's 2023 Cost of a Data Breach Report found that organizations with extensive use of security AI and automation experienced an average of $1.76 million lower breach costs than organizations with limited or no such capabilities [20]. The 2024 report reinforced this trend, showing that organizations with mature automation capabilities continued to reduce breach lifecycle timelines and operational costs compared with organizations that relied on slower manual processes [21]. This supports the broader point that stronger visibility and response maturity reduce operational impact, even though technology alone does not eliminate User Risk.

6. Case Study: User Risk Within RMF, Evidence from the Anthem Data Breach

The 2015 breach of Anthem Inc. exposed approximately 78.8 million records, including names, Social Security numbers, and birthdates. Attackers gained access through compromised user credentials, likely obtained via phishing, and operated the network undetected for an extended period.

Post-incident findings confirmed that the attackers

maintained persistent access for weeks, using valid credentials to move laterally and extract sensitive data. In 2018, the Office for Civil Rights (OCR) issued a $16 million HIPAA settlement, citing failures in risk analysis and insufficient safeguards [48].

From an RMF perspective, this incident reflects a gap between control implementation and control performance under real-world User Risk.

RMF Control Mapping and User Risk Exposure

IA, Identification and Authentication

- Controls were implemented and operational
- Compromised credentials enabled valid access
- RMF verifies authentication mechanisms, not user susceptibility to compromise

AC, Access Control

- Access policies enforced as designed
- Legitimate credentials enabled large-scale data access
- RMF validates permissions, not how User Risk expands effective access

AU, Audit and Accountability

- Logging capabilities were present
- Anomalous activity was not detected in time
- RMF confirms logging, not active behavioral analysis

IR, Incident Response

- Response processes existed
- Detection lag allowed prolonged attacker dwell time
- RMF assesses plans, not real-time responsiveness to user-driven anomalies

AT, Awareness and Training

- Training requirements were met

- Initial compromise likely resulted from phishing
- RMF tracks completion, not behavioral effectiveness

Post-Breach Technology Response

- Anthem implemented targeted improvements to increase visibility into User Risk:
- Expanded SIEM capabilities to correlate and detect anomalous activity
- Broadened multi-factor authentication for privileged and remote access
- Deployed User Risk analytics to baseline and flag deviations
- Strengthened data loss prevention controls on sensitive data movement
- Enhanced phishing simulations to measure user decision performance

Operational Insight

- Prior to the breach, RMF evidence would have supported an Authorization to Operate:
- Controls implemented
- Policies enforced
- Training completed
- Logging enabled

The failure occurred within the boundary of authorized user activity. The corrective actions did not eliminate User Risk. They increased its observability:

- User actions became attributable
- Behavioral deviations became detectable
- Detection and response timelines improved

This case establishes a clear principle:

System authorization reflects control implementation. System trust reflects how users behave within those controls.

7. Conclusion

Technology strengthens User Risk management when it improves visibility, supports enforcement, and enables continuous monitoring and response to behavioral risk [3], [30]. It is most valuable when it complements policy, training, and governance rather than substituting for them. The next chapter examines how User Risk can be mapped to RMF and where the remaining evidence gaps persist.

Closing Leadership Question

How do you use technology to observe, constrain, and respond to user-driven risk in your environment?

Chapter 9. Mapping User Risk to RMF

1. Introduction

RMF already contains everything necessary to govern User Risk, except a method for measuring it. It supports categorization, control selection, implementation, assessment, authorization, and continuous monitoring [31]. What it does not explicitly measure is how human decision variability affects control effectiveness during operational use.

This chapter explains how User Risk can be mapped to RMF, where evidence gaps remain, and how organizations can begin addressing them.

2. Aligning User Risk with RMF

Mapping User Risk to RMF begins by identifying the User Risks most likely to influence system trust and then linking those behaviors to existing risk assessment and management processes.

User Risk should be documented alongside technical risk. Each identified behavior should include operational context, potential impact, and the likelihood that it could degrade control effectiveness.

Common evidence gaps emerge quickly. Organizations often have limited visibility into user activity patterns, inconsistent policy enforcement, and uneven reporting practices. These gaps make it difficult to assess user-related exposure with the same precision applied to technical controls.

Organizations can reduce those gaps by implementing more consistent monitoring, documenting user-related risk factors, and using defined indicators to reduce subjectivity in behavioral assessment.

3. Why RMF Does Not Produce User Risk Indicators

RMF attempts to influence User Risk through controls such as training, access restrictions, policy acknowledgments, and reporting procedures. These mechanisms shape expectations. They do not directly measure behavior.

Technical controls generate measurable outputs. Vulnerability scanners produce findings. Configuration tools produce compliance scores. Continuous monitoring produces operational metrics.

User behavior produces far fewer direct indicators. Training completion records confirm that instruction occurred. Policy acknowledgments confirm awareness. Neither confirms the quality of decisions users make during operations.

This limitation matters because the human element remains central to breach activity. RMF verifies that controls are implemented and operating as intended. It does not explicitly measure how users apply those controls under operational pressure.

4. User Risk Indicators

RMF evaluates technical safeguards through measurable evidence. Vulnerability scans identify weaknesses, configuration assessments verify compliance, and continuous monitoring provides operational data that supports authorization decisions. These technical artifacts allow organizations to evaluate the integrity of implemented controls with a high degree of confidence.

Human behavior produces far fewer measurable artifacts. Training records, policy acknowledgments, and access approvals confirm that required activities occurred, but they do not reveal how users exercise judgment while interacting with security controls during normal operations.

This distinction creates a fundamental evidence gap. Organizations can verify that safeguards exist and function as intended, yet have limited visibility into how user decisions influence those safeguards after systems enter operational use.

User Risk Indicators help close that gap. Rather than measuring technical performance, they measure behavioral conditions that influence control effectiveness. Organizations routinely use performance measures to evaluate cybersecurity programs, yet comparable measures for operational User Risk remain largely undeveloped [30].

Table 1 illustrates examples of behavioral indicators that organizations may begin collecting today [2], [17]. These indicators are not intended to replace existing RMF evidence. They complement it by providing visibility into the human decisions that technical assessments cannot observe.

User Risk Indicator	Description
Privilege escalation frequency	Rate of elevated access requests
Policy override events	Instances where safeguards are bypassed
Phishing susceptibility rate	Percentage of users who engage malicious links
Incident reporting delay	Time between the event and reporting
Authentication approval anomalies	Unusual approval patterns in MFA prompts

Table 1. User Risk Indicators

Unlike technical findings, these indicators rarely provide meaningful insight in isolation. Their value emerges when they are analyzed collectively and observed over time.

This progression from individual observations to governance decisions is illustrated through the User Risk Measurement Lifecycle.

5. From Behavioral Evidence to Risk Decisions

Technical controls already follow a well-established measurement process. Vulnerability scanners generate findings. Findings are analyzed, prioritized, and incorporated into risk decisions. User Risk requires a similar discipline.

The User Risk Measurement Lifecycle, shown in Figure 2, provides a structured approach for transforming observed behavior into governance-relevant evidence.

The lifecycle begins with Behavioral Evidence, the observable actions users perform while interacting with systems. Examples include approving an unexpected multi-factor authentication request, delaying the reporting of suspicious activity, repeatedly requesting elevated privileges, bypassing established approval processes, or ignoring security alerts. Individually, these actions rarely establish elevated risk. They simply represent observable operational behavior.

Behavioral evidence becomes meaningful when it is transformed into User Risk Indicators. Rather than focusing on isolated events, indicators measure recurring behavioral conditions such as privilege escalation frequency, phishing susceptibility, policy override frequency, authentication anomalies, or reporting delays. Indicators provide measurable signals that can be compared across users, teams, and operational environments.

Figure 2. User Risk Measurement Lifecycle

Once indicators have been collected, organizations evaluate them through trend analysis. Just as vulnerability management relies on recurring scans to identify deteriorating security posture, behavioral indicators become valuable when examined over time. Increasing phishing susceptibility, longer reporting delays, or rising policy override events may reveal emerging operational risks long before they contribute to a security incident.

As behavioral measurement matures, these trends may eventually support User Risk scoring. Standardized scoring methods do not currently exist within RMF, but behavioral indicators provide the foundation from which future scoring approaches may emerge [31]. The objective is not to reduce Human Judgment to a single number. It is to summarize behavioral conditions in a manner that supports consistent comparison and informed governance decisions.

The final stage of the lifecycle integrates these observations into risk decisions. Behavioral evidence does not replace existing RMF artifacts. It complements them. Technical evidence demonstrates that safeguards have been implemented correctly. Behavioral evidence demonstrates how those safeguards perform when users interact with them during daily operations.

Together, these evidence sources provide a more complete view of operational risk.

Figure 2 extends the Operational Trust Model introduced in Chapter 5 by illustrating how Behavioral Evidence can be transformed into governance-relevant information. Technical assessments provide evidence of control reliability. User Risk measurement provides evidence of Human Judgment. Combined, they offer decision-makers a more complete understanding of Operational Trust.

Organizations cannot eliminate human decision variability. They can, however, observe it, measure it, monitor it over time, and incorporate it into authorization decisions. That transition from assumption to observable evidence represents the next practical evolution of cybersecurity governance.

6. Case Study: Colonial Pipeline and the Operational Consequences of User Risk

The Colonial Pipeline ransomware attack in May 2021 demonstrates how weaknesses in routine access management can escalate into consequences far beyond the compromised account. Attackers gained access to Colonial Pipeline's network through a legacy VPN account that was no longer actively used. The account's credentials had been compromised, and multi-factor authentication was not enabled.

Once ransomware affected the company's business network, Colonial Pipeline shut down pipeline operations as a precaution. The disruption affected a system responsible for transporting a substantial share of the fuel consumed along the East Coast, contributing to fuel shortages, panic buying, price increases, and emergency government actions. What began as compromised remote access therefore became an operational and economic event.

The incident is particularly relevant to User Risk because the initial weakness was not simply the absence of cybersecurity technology. The organization had security controls and access-management processes. The exposure involved decisions surrounding the lifecycle of an account: whether an unused account remained active, whether remote access required multi-factor authentication, whether credentials associated with dormant access were adequately governed, and whether access privileges were continuously reviewed. These are administrative and human decisions that determine whether technical controls remain effective over time.

Colonial Pipeline paid the attackers 75 bitcoin, valued at approximately $4.4 million at the time. The Department of Justice later recovered 63.7 bitcoin, then valued at more than $2.3 million [6], [49]. Pipeline operations resumed following the disruption, while the incident prompted broader scrutiny of cybersecurity practices within the nation's critical infrastructure.

Viewed through the User Risk framework, Colonial Pipeline illustrates the difference between having controls and sustaining their effectiveness. Account management and authentication controls can exist on paper and in system architecture, yet their protective value depends on people consistently disabling unnecessary accounts, enforcing stronger authentication, reviewing access, and responding to changing operational conditions.

The incident therefore represents more than a ransomware case. It demonstrates how an apparently routine administrative condition can become consequential when Human Judgment, control execution, and operational dependency intersect. The technical safeguards mattered, but so did the decisions governing them.

7. Mapping User Behavior to RMF Security Controls

User Risk can be mapped to specific RMF control families by identifying the decisions most likely to influence control effectiveness.

Access Control: User behavior affects credential management, privilege use, and authentication practices. Controls such as IA-2 and AC-3 remain technically necessary, but their practical effectiveness still depends on how users handle approval requests, passwords, and elevated access.

Awareness and Training: AT-2 requires awareness

training tailored to organizational risk [32]. Completion demonstrates participation, not the quality of decisions under operational conditions [42].

Incident Response: IR-4 depends in part on how quickly users recognize and report suspicious activity. Reporting speed and escalation behavior become meaningful operational indicators of user-driven risk during incidents [20].

System and Communications Protection: Controls such as SC-7 define protections for communications and boundaries, but users still determine whether approved channels are used correctly in practice.

Media Protection: Controls such as MP-4 depend on how users store, handle, and dispose of information-bearing media in daily operations.

8. Interim Approaches for Organizations

Organizations can begin operationalizing User Risk through practical, defensible measures.

Comprehensive training programs remain important, but they should be reinforced with decision-based exercises and role-specific scenarios. Finance teams, administrators, analysts, and managers do not face the same decision environment and should not receive identical training treatment.

User-friendly policy also matters. When security expectations are clear, accessible, and operationally realistic, adherence improves. Feedback mechanisms can then be used to update both training and policy based on what users actually encounter during operations, improving reporting behavior and organizational awareness [2].

9. Conclusion

Mapping User Risk to RMF helps organizations identify gaps in Behavioral Evidence, connect user actions to control families, and strengthen risk decisions that would otherwise rely on assumptions. The next chapter turns to operationalizing User Risk by moving from awareness to accountability.

Closing Leadership Question

What strategies do you use to ensure user decisions preserve trust within your RMF implementation?

Part IV. Operationalizing User Risk

Chapter 10. From Awareness to Accountability

1. Introduction

Awareness alone does not create accountability [42]. People are rarely judged by what they know. Organizations are judged by what their people do.

This chapter examines how organizations can move from informing users about risk to holding them accountable for the security outcomes of their decisions.

2. Frameworks for Transitioning to Accountability

Transitioning to accountability requires structures that assign ownership, clarify expectations, and reinforce responsibility for security outcomes [2].

The Accountability Pyramid

Accountability rarely develops through policy alone. Organizations generally progress through recognizable stages in which awareness gradually evolves into ownership of security outcomes. One way to visualize that progression is through the Accountability Pyramid.

- **Awareness:** At this foundational level, organizations educate employees about potential cybersecurity risks, security policies, and protocols. Awareness programs must be role-specific, focusing on the particular security challenges faced by different employee groups.
- **Engagement:** This middle layer emphasizes engaging employees in dialogues about security practices and encouraging interaction. Workshops, security games, and open discussions allow employees to voice their concerns and share security experiences, enhancing collective understanding.
- **Accountability:** The pinnacle of the pyramid builds a culture where every employee understands their role in maintaining security. Clear articulation of security roles, regular performance reviews that include security

metrics, and recognition of employees demonstrating accountability can solidify this culture.

The Security Responsibility Framework

Another effective framework for transitioning to accountability is the Security Responsibility Framework, which outlines key responsibilities at all organizational levels:

- **Senior Leadership:** Sets the tone for accountability through shared vision, resource allocation, and commitment to security measures.
- **Management:** Responsible for translating policies into specific tasks for teams, including regular assessments of security practices and encouraging accountability among employees.
- **Employees:** Must feel empowered to make decisions regarding security practices. Clear guidelines and support for employees help inculcate a sense of ownership over security responsibilities.

3. Case Studies of Successful Shifts

These incidents are selected because they demonstrate documented instances where human decisions directly influenced control effectiveness and operational outcomes.

Case Study: Integrating User Risk into Cybersecurity Practice, Lessons from the Target Data Breach

The 2013 breach of Target Corporation compromised approximately 40 million payment card records and 70 million customer records. The attack originated through compromised credentials from a third-party HVAC vendor, which were used to access Target's internal network.

Attackers moved laterally, deployed malware to point-of-sale systems, and exfiltrated data over several weeks. Notably, security tools generated alerts during the intrusion, but human response failures allowed the activity to continue [51].

The breach resulted in over $200 million in total costs and significant reputational damage, forcing leadership changes and triggering enterprise-wide security reforms.

RMF Control Mapping and User Risk Exposure

IA, Identification and Authentication

- Vendor credentials were valid but compromised
- Gap: RMF verifies authentication controls, not third-party User Risk or credential exposure

AC, Access Control

- Vendor access exceeded operational necessity
- Gap: RMF validates access assignment, not how User Risk and vendor relationships expand attack paths

AU, Audit and Accountability

- Security systems generated actionable alerts
- Gap: RMF confirms logging and alerting, not whether users act on alerts effectively

IR, Incident Response

- Alerts were not escalated or acted upon in time
- Gap: RMF assesses response plans, not real-world execution under operational pressure

AT, Awareness and Training

- Personnel failed to recognize or act on critical alerts
- Gap: RMF tracks training completion, not decision-making performance in live scenarios

Post-Breach Integration of User Risk

Following the breach, Target implemented a

comprehensive transformation that directly integrated User Risk into cybersecurity operations:

- Strengthened third-party access controls and network segmentation
- Expanded continuous monitoring and real-time alert escalation processes
- Increased investment in security operations center staffing and training
- Implemented enhanced security awareness programs focused on detection and reporting
- Introduced stricter governance over vendor access and credential management

Measurable Outcomes

- Reduced vendor access exposure through tighter segmentation and credential controls
- Improved response times to security alerts within the SOC
- Increased organizational focus on user accountability in cybersecurity operations

While specific internal metrics were not publicly disclosed, industry analysis confirmed that Target's post-breach investments significantly improved detection and response capabilities and reduced similar risk exposure [51].

What RMF Would Have Reported Pre-Breach

- Authentication controls implemented
- Access controls defined
- Logging and alerting systems operational
- Incident response plans documented
- Training requirements satisfied
- The system likely maintained an Authorization to Operate.

What Was Missing

- Measurement of third-party User Risk
- Validation of user response to security alerts
- Behavioral analysis of access patterns across vendor accounts
- Real-time accountability for human decision points

Operational Insight

The breach did not result from the absence of controls. It resulted from how users and third parties operated within those controls. Target's response did not focus solely on adding technology. It focused on integrating User Risk into operational security:

- User actions became part of the detection model
- Alert response became a measurable performance variable
- Third-party behavior became a managed risk domain

This case reinforces a core principle:

Controls define what is allowed. User behavior determines what actually happens.

Case Study: Identity Verification and User Risk, Lessons from the MGM Resorts Cyberattack

In September 2023, MGM Resorts International experienced a major cyber incident that disrupted hotel operations, casino systems, and digital services across multiple properties. Slot machines were disabled, reservation systems failed, and customer-facing services were degraded for several days.

Public reporting and company disclosures indicate that attackers used social engineering to impersonate an employee and successfully engage the IT help desk. The attackers obtained access, escalated privileges, and moved laterally within the environment.

MGM reported an estimated financial impact of approximately $100 million due to operational disruption and recovery efforts [54], [17], [53].

RMF Control Mapping and User Risk Exposure

IA, Identification and Authentication

- Identity verification relied on help desk procedures
- Gap: RMF validates authentication mechanisms, not the effectiveness of human identity verification during support interactions

AC, Access Control

- Privileged access was granted following help desk interaction
- Gap: RMF confirms access enforcement, not the decision quality at the point of access approval

IA-5 / IA-8 Context, Authenticator Management and Identification

- Account recovery and reset processes were exploited
- Gap: RMF documents procedures, not resistance to social engineering

AT, Awareness and Training

- Help desk personnel were targeted through impersonation
- Gap: RMF tracks training completion, not performance under live social engineering conditions

AU, Audit and Accountability

- Actions were logged after access was granted
- Gap: RMF confirms logging, not prevention of high-risk actions initiated through user deception

IR, Incident Response

- Organization responded after operational disruption

became visible

- Gap: RMF evaluates response plans, not speed of detection tied to user-driven access events

Post-Incident Control and Process Adjustments

Following the incident, MGM and industry peers emphasized stronger controls at the human interaction layer:

- Enhanced identity verification procedures for help desk and account recovery workflows
- Increased use of phishing-resistant multi-factor authentication methods
- Additional restrictions on privilege escalation through support channels
- Expanded monitoring of account changes and privileged access events
- Targeted training focused on real-time social engineering resistance

Measurable Outcomes

While detailed internal metrics were not publicly released, industry reporting and disclosures indicate:

- Increased adoption of phishing-resistant MFA across critical systems
- Greater scrutiny of help desk identity verification processes
- Elevated focus on user interaction points as high-risk control boundaries

What RMF Would Have Reported Pre-Incident

- Authentication mechanisms implemented
- Access control policies enforced
- Account management procedures documented
- Training completed
- Logging enabled
- Incident response plans established

- System likely maintained an Authorization to Operate.

What Was Missing

- Measurement of identity verification effectiveness during human interactions
- Validation of help desk decision-making under social engineering pressure
- Real-time controls on privilege escalation initiated through user requests
- Behavioral detection at the point of access approval

Operational Insight

The attack did not begin with a technical exploit. It began with a human interaction. Controls were present. Identity systems existed. Access processes were defined. The failure occurred at the moment a user approved access based on a deceptive request.

The corrective focus is clear:

- Identity verification must be treated as a high-risk decision point
- User interactions must be measurable and monitored
- Access approval must include behavioral validation, not just procedural compliance

This case reinforces a critical principle:

- Authentication verifies credentials. Users decide whether to trust them.

Case Study: Third-Party Identity Trust and User Risk, Lessons from the Caesars Entertainment Cyberattack

In September 2023, Caesars Entertainment disclosed a cybersecurity incident in which attackers used social engineering to compromise credentials from an outsourced IT support provider. The attackers used this access to infiltrate company systems and exfiltrate sensitive data, including customer loyalty program information.

Company filings with the U.S. Securities and Exchange Commission confirmed that Caesars paid approximately $15 million to prevent further disclosure of stolen data [55].

The initial access vector was not a system vulnerability. It was identity manipulation within a trusted supply chain relationship.

RMF Control Mapping and User Risk Exposure

SR, Supply Chain Risk Management

- Third-party provider was vetted, authorized, and integrated into operations
- Gap: RMF evaluates supplier controls and governance, not the behavior of individual users within the supplier environment

IA, Identification and Authentication

- Vendor credentials were valid but obtained through deception
- Gap: RMF verifies authentication mechanisms, not resistance to impersonation

AC, Access Control

- Third-party access enabled entry into internal systems
- Gap: RMF confirms access provisioning, not decision quality at the point of access approval

IA-5 / Account Management Context

- Credential handling and reset processes were exploited
- Gap: RMF documents procedures, not resilience

under social engineering pressure

AT, Awareness and Training

- Third-party personnel were targeted and deceived
- Gap: RMF tracks training requirements, not effectiveness across vendor users

AU, Audit and Accountability

- Activity was logged after access occurred
- Gap: RMF confirms logging, not prevention of misuse through trusted accounts

IR, Incident Response

- Response initiated after data exfiltration
- Gap: RMF evaluates response plans, not detection at the moment of compromised user interaction

What RMF Would Have Reported Pre-Incident

- Supplier assessed and approved under SR controls
- Third-party access authorized and documented
- Authentication and access controls implemented
- Account management procedures defined
- Training requirements established
- Logging enabled
- Incident response plans in place
- System likely maintained an Authorization to Operate.

What Was Missing

Caesars disclosed that it took steps to contain and remediate the incident, but the cited filing did not publicly disclose details of specific corrective measures [55]. As a result, the case provides stronger evidence of the initial access failure and its consequences than of the specific controls implemented afterward.

- Measurement of third-party user susceptibility to social engineering

- Validation of identity verification under adversarial conditions
- Behavioral monitoring of vendor users as a distinct risk population
- Controls to limit impact of compromised third-party credentials

Operational Insight

The attack did not exploit a breakdown in supply chain governance. It exploited a breakdown in human decision-making within that supply chain. The supplier was trusted. The access was authorized. The procedures were followed.

The failure occurred when a user inside the trusted boundary accepted a false identity.

This case establishes a clear principle:

Supply chain controls define who is trusted. User behavior determines whether that trust holds.

Case Study: Credential Management and Authentication Enforcement, Lessons from the Change Healthcare Cyberattack

In February 2024, Change Healthcare, a subsidiary of UnitedHealth Group, suffered a ransomware attack that disrupted healthcare claims processing across the United States. The outage affected pharmacies, hospitals, and providers, delaying prescriptions, billing, and payment workflows nationwide.

Public reporting and congressional testimony confirmed that attackers gained access through compromised credentials. Multi-factor authentication was not enabled on the affected system at the time of intrusion [58]. UnitedHealth later stated that its policies required MFA on externally facing applications, but the compromised legacy Change Healthcare server had not yet been brought into compliance with those standards [58].

The operational impact extended beyond a single enterprise, affecting a significant portion of U.S. healthcare transaction processing infrastructure.

RMF Control Mapping and User Risk Exposure

IA, Identification and Authentication

- Authentication relied on credentials without MFA enforcement
- Gap: RMF verifies authentication mechanisms exist, not whether strong authentication is consistently enforced

IA-2 / IA-5 Context, Authenticator Management

- Credential-based access was sufficient for system entry
- Gap: RMF documents authenticator requirements, not whether users and administrators enforce them across all systems

AC, Access Control

- Access granted through valid credentials
- Gap: RMF confirms access control structure, not risk of credential compromise

CM, Configuration Management

- MFA was not enabled on a critical system
- Gap: RMF validates configuration baselines, not the enforcement of security configurations across operational environments

AT, Awareness and Training

- Credential compromise indicates exposure to phishing or credential theft
- Gap: RMF tracks training completion, not resistance

to credential-based attacks

AU, Audit and Accountability

- Detection occurred after compromise and disruption
- Gap: RMF confirms logging, not real-time detection of credential misuse

IR, Incident Response

- Response initiated after widespread operational disruption
- Gap: RMF evaluates response plans, not speed of detection tied to user-driven access events

SR, Supply Chain Risk Management

- Change Healthcare operated as a critical third-party service provider within the healthcare ecosystem
- Gap: RMF evaluates supplier governance, not the behavioral and configuration risks within high-impact service providers

What RMF Would Have Reported Pre-Incident

- Authentication controls implemented
- Access controls enforced
- Configuration management policies defined
- Supplier role established within the healthcare ecosystem
- Training requirements satisfied
- Logging enabled
- Incident response plans documented
- System likely maintained an Authorization to Operate.

What Was Missing

- Enforcement of multi-factor authentication on all critical systems
- Measurement of credential compromise risk
- Validation of configuration decisions by system

owners

- Behavioral monitoring of authentication events
- Risk assessment of high-impact service providers as user-driven environments

Following the attack, UnitedHealth Group reported continued efforts to strengthen its cybersecurity defenses, including broader deployment of multi-factor authentication on externally facing applications, continuous monitoring and assessment, and work with external cybersecurity firms to improve security controls. The response reinforced the importance of validating that required authentication safeguards are implemented consistently across operational systems [58].

The incident also illustrates an important distinction for User Risk measurement. A policy requiring MFA is administrative evidence. Verification that MFA is actually enabled and enforced on applicable systems is operational evidence. The difference can determine whether compromised credentials result in an unsuccessful access attempt or a major operational incident.

Operational Insight

UnitedHealth later stated that its policies required MFA on externally facing applications, but the compromised legacy Change Healthcare server had not yet complied with those standards [58].

The breach did not result from the absence of authentication controls. It resulted from failure to enforce them. Credentials were valid. Access was authorized. Controls were defined.

The Change Healthcare attack shows that documenting a security requirement is not the same as implementing it. MFA was a known security safeguard, yet the affected remote-access system did not enforce it. The resulting exposure was therefore not simply a technical weakness. It reflected a gap between expected control implementation and actual operational practice.

From a User Risk perspective, this distinction is critical. RMF evidence may demonstrate that an organization has established authentication requirements, policies, and responsibilities. Behavioral Evidence asks the next question: Were the people responsible for implementing and maintaining those safeguards actually doing so?

This case reinforces a central principle:

- Authentication policy defines requirements. User action determines whether those requirements are enforced.

4. Statistics and Research Findings

Threat intelligence and incident analyses consistently show that credential misuse, phishing engagement, and user-driven configuration errors remain among the most common causes of system compromise, reinforcing that human behavior is a persistent driver of cyber incidents [8], [9], [44].

Research also shows that organizations with stronger security cultures experience lower rates of policy violations and faster incident reporting, reinforcing that accountability frameworks produce measurable behavioral outcomes [23].

Organizations that conduct repeated phishing simulations and awareness exercises can also observe measurable changes in reporting behavior. Proofpoint's 2023 State of the Phish reported measurable improvements in phishing reporting rates alongside persistent user susceptibility to simulated attacks [40].

5. Scenarios and Hypothetical Situations

Consider an employee in accounts payable who receives an urgent message that appears to come from a senior executive requesting a funds transfer. The employee is under deadline pressure and bypasses verification procedures. This is not simply an awareness issue. It is an accountability issue shaped by role pressure, urgency, and unclear enforcement.

Consider also a software engineer who repeatedly accesses corporate systems through unsecured public Wi-Fi because convenience outweighs perceived risk. The behavior persists until a security event occurs. Again, the issue is not only knowledge. It is the absence of operational accountability.

6. Discussion on Technology Interface

User interfaces play a significant role in influencing employee decision-making regarding cybersecurity practices. Poorly designed interfaces can frustrate users, leading them to bypass essential security protocols, particularly under cognitive load [10]. Organizations should invest in User Experience (UX) design to ensure security tools are accessible and intuitive, ultimately empowering users to follow security practices without frustration.

Behavioral nudges, such as reminder notifications for password updates or prompts during potential security events, can reinforce positive decision-making and improve compliance behavior [2]. For instance, a well-designed authentication interface should guide users through multi-factor authentication, emphasizing its importance while simplifying the user experience.

7. Conclusion

Moving from awareness to accountability is

essential for building a durable cybersecurity culture and aligning User Risk with organizational risk expectations [2]. Frameworks that emphasize ownership make responsible security behavior more enforceable and more sustainable.

Leadership must commit to establishing accountability at every level, ensuring that all employees understand their critical roles in maintaining security. As the consequences of human error become clearer, accountability becomes a practical requirement for organizational resilience.

Closing Leadership Question

What specific steps have you taken to ensure every user in your organization is accountable for the security outcomes of their decisions?

Chapter 11. Measuring Accountability Effectiveness

1. Introduction

Accountability only matters if it can be observed and evaluated. Organizations need ways to measure whether accountability initiatives are changing behavior and improving outcomes.

Earlier chapters established that RMF contains behavioral controls but lacks behavioral indicators. Measurement methods address that gap. This chapter examines how accountability can be measured through key performance indicators, evaluation techniques, and operational examples.

It also addresses the practical challenges of measurement and the strategies organizations can use to address them.

2. Key Performance Indicators (KPIs)

As described in the Operational Trust Model earlier in this book, system trust depends on both the reliability of technical safeguards and the quality of human decisions made when interacting with those safeguards.

Measuring accountability in cybersecurity requires key performance indicators that align with security objectives and reveal whether behavior is actually improving. No single metric can determine whether accountability is improving. Effective measurement requires observing multiple indicators that collectively reveal whether users are making better security decisions over time. The following performance measures provide that broader perspective.

- **Incident Response Time:** Measures the time required to detect, respond to, and contain security incidents. Faster response times are associated with reduced breach impact. IBM Security reported in 2023 that organizations with mature incident response capabilities and extensive security automation experienced, on average, $1.76 million lower breach costs [20]. The company's 2024 findings continued to show that faster detection and containment remain strongly associated with reduced financial impact [21].

- **Phishing Simulation Success Rates:** Measures the percentage of users who correctly identify and report simulated phishing attempts. This metric reflects applied judgment under realistic conditions. Proofpoint's 2023 research found that phishing reporting rates increased to 17%, up from 15% in 2021, demonstrating measurable behavioral improvement through repeated simulation and training [40].
- **Training Completion Rates:** Measures participation in required security awareness training. NIST SP 800-53 control AT-2 requires organizations to provide role-based training; however, completion alone does not indicate improved decision-making or reduced risk [32]. This metric should therefore be used as a baseline indicator, not a measure of effectiveness.
- **Security Policy Violations:** Tracks the number and frequency of deviations from established security policies. Continuous monitoring guidance emphasizes tracking control adherence over time to identify trends and areas of increased risk [3]. A reduction in violations may indicate improved behavioral alignment with security expectations.
- **User Engagement and Reporting Behavior:** Measures user participation in security processes, including incident reporting, escalation, and feedback. NIST Cybersecurity Framework 2.0 highlights governance and organizational culture as critical components of cybersecurity risk management, reinforcing that user engagement is a necessary condition for effective security outcomes [34].

These measurement practices also reinforce the accountability structures introduced in the previous chapter. Metrics such as reporting speed, phishing response rates, policy violations, and escalation behavior help organizations evaluate whether users are progressing through the Accountability Pyramid from awareness to engagement to operational accountability. They also provide evidence that the Security Responsibility Framework is functioning as intended by showing whether leadership, management, and individual users are meeting their assigned security responsibilities. Without measurement, these frameworks remain conceptual models rather than operational governance tools.

3. Evaluation Techniques

Employing evaluation techniques helps organizations assess the effectiveness of accountability initiatives. Effective approaches include:

- **Surveys and Questionnaires:** Regular surveys can assess employee understanding of security policies, perceived accountability, and willingness to report issues. Anonymous reporting mechanisms are specifically recommended to improve reporting quality and reduce fear of reprisal. CISA emphasizes that organizations should enable anonymous reporting channels to strengthen incident detection and encourage participation [5].
- **Performance Reviews:** Integrating security responsibilities into performance evaluations reinforces accountability by linking behavior to organizational expectations. NIST highlights that organizations should define roles and responsibilities clearly and ensure personnel are held accountable for assigned security duties [31]. Performance alignment ensures that security

is treated as an operational responsibility, not a secondary task.

- **Regular Security Audits:** Periodic audits assess compliance with security policies, control effectiveness, and implementation consistency. NIST guidance on continuous monitoring stresses the importance of ongoing assessment to identify control degradation and emerging risk conditions over time [30]. Audit findings provide measurable evidence of whether expected behaviors are being followed in practice.
- **Incident Post-Mortems**: Post-incident analysis evaluates what occurred, why it occurred, and how decisions influenced outcomes. Reviews of the Equifax Data Breach showed that failure to remediate a known vulnerability contributed to the exposure of approximately 147 million individuals' data, demonstrating how delayed action and breakdowns in responsibility can lead to large-scale impact [14]. Post-mortems, therefore, serve as a critical mechanism for identifying accountability gaps and improving future response.

4. Detailed Examples and Case Studies

Case studies help show how accountability failures translate into operational and financial consequences.

Case Study: Accountability and User Risk, Lessons from the Equifax Data Breach

The 2017 Equifax breach exposed the sensitive data of approximately 147 million individuals, including Social Security numbers, birthdates, and addresses. The attack exploited a known vulnerability in Apache Struts (CVE-2017-5638) for which a patch had been available for over two months prior to the breach [36].

Investigations confirmed that Equifax failed to identify and remediate the vulnerable system in a timely manner. Attackers gained access in May 2017 and maintained a presence until July 2017. Detection occurred only after significant data exfiltration had already taken place.

The Federal Trade Commission, in coordination with other agencies, later announced a settlement of up to $700 million, citing failures in patch management, asset visibility, and governance [14]. Congressional findings further emphasized breakdowns in accountability, communication, and role clarity across the organization [50].

RMF Control Mapping and Accountability Breakdown

SI, System and Information Integrity

- Patch for a critical vulnerability was not applied
- Gap: RMF verifies patch processes exist, not whether responsible users execute them within required timelines

CM, Configuration Management

- Incomplete asset inventory led to missed systems
- Gap: RMF validates configuration baselines, not accuracy of system ownership and tracking by users

RA, Risk Assessment

- Known vulnerability was not effectively prioritized or mitigated
- Gap: RMF assesses risk processes, not whether users act on identified risks

PL, Planning (Roles and Responsibilities)

- Lack of clear accountability for patching and system ownership
- Gap: RMF documents roles, not enforcement of responsibility across teams

AU, Audit and Accountability

- Monitoring tools failed to detect ongoing exploitation in time
- Gap: RMF confirms logging, not whether users review and act on audit data

IR, Incident Response

- Delayed detection and response extended attacker dwell time
- Gap: RMF evaluates response plans, not execution speed tied to user action

AT, Awareness and Training

- Personnel failed to act on known vulnerability alerts
- Gap: RMF tracks training completion, not operational decision-making

Post-Incident Accountability Integration

Following the breach, Equifax implemented structural changes focused on accountability and execution:

- Centralized patch management with defined ownership and timelines
- Improved asset inventory and system visibility
- Strengthened governance over vulnerability management processes
- Expanded training focused on operational accountability, not just awareness
- Enhanced executive oversight of cybersecurity risk decisions

Measurable Outcomes

- Improved patching timelines for critical vulnerabilities
- Increased visibility into system ownership and accountability

- Strengthened governance and oversight of remediation actions

Regulatory findings confirmed that remediation efforts focused on enforcing accountability and improving execution of existing controls.

What RMF Would Have Reported Pre-Breach

- Patch management processes documented
- Configuration management policies established
- Risk assessment procedures defined
- Roles and responsibilities assigned
- Logging and monitoring enabled
- Training completed
- System likely maintained an Authorization to Operate.

What Was Missing

- Accountability for patch execution
- Validation of asset ownership and system coverage
- Measurement of remediation timeliness
- Enforcement of user responsibility for known risks

Operational Insight

The breach did not occur because patching controls were absent. It occurred because users responsible for executing those controls did not act in time.

Equifax's corrective actions did not introduce new categories of controls. They enforced accountability within existing ones:

- Responsibility became explicit and measurable
- Execution timelines became monitored
- Ownership gaps were reduced

This case reinforces a core principle:

Controls define required actions. Accountability determines whether those actions occur.

5. Research Basis for Behavioral Measurement

Research on information security behavior provides additional support for measuring accountability beyond administrative compliance. The Human Aspects of Information Security Questionnaire, or HAIS-Q, demonstrates that security-related knowledge, attitudes, and behaviors can be systematically assessed rather than treated as intangible characteristics [42].

This distinction is important for User Risk because training completion, policy acknowledgment, and control implementation indicate that security requirements have been addressed. At the same time, Behavioral Evidence provides insight into how those requirements influence operational behavior.

6. Hypothetical Scenarios

The following scenarios illustrate how accountability failures surface through measurement patterns rather than individual incidents.

Consider an organization that tracks security training completion rates, phishing simulation results, and policy acknowledgment logs as part of its accountability framework. Over two consecutive quarters, completion rates hold steady at 94%. However, phishing simulation failure rates rise from 11% to 23% across the same population. No single employee triggered a reportable incident. The KPI trend, not an individual event, is the signal. Without a measurement layer tracking behavioral outcomes alongside administrative completion, the organization would have seen a compliant workforce on paper while Operational Trust degraded in practice. This is precisely the gap the Operational Trust Model identifies.

Now consider a second organization that uses access log anomalies as a behavioral indicator. An administrator's account shows a pattern of privileged access requests outside normal working hours, spanning three weeks. The requests are within policy limits. Each individual action passes technical control checks. No alert fires. The pattern only becomes visible when behavioral baseline data is reviewed at the monthly accountability review. At that point, the organization has a documented trend, a timestamped record, and an evidence-based basis for intervention, none of which would exist without a formal measurement structure.

These scenarios demonstrate that accountability failure rarely announces itself through a single dramatic event. It accumulates as a measurable drift between expected behavior and observed behavior over time. Organizations that rely on incident response alone will always be responding after the fact. Organizations with a functioning measurement framework detect the drift first.

7. Best Practices for Organizations

Best practices for enhancing employee accountability include a multifaceted approach to training and continuous engagement. Recommended strategies incorporate varied methods effective in raising cybersecurity awareness:

- **Interactive Training Programs:** Interactive and scenario-based training improves engagement and retention by requiring users to apply judgment rather than passively consume information. NIST emphasizes that security awareness programs should be role-based and tailored to organizational risks, including practical exercises that reflect real-world conditions [32]. Interactive training shifts focus from knowledge acquisition to decision-making.
- **Regular Security Drills:** Simulated exercises,

including phishing scenarios and incident response drills, allow organizations to test User Risk under realistic conditions. These exercises provide measurable indicators such as reporting rates, response time, and error frequency. Proofpoint's 2023 research shows that repeated phishing simulations can improve user reporting behavior over time, making drills a practical way to reinforce secure actions [40].

- **Clear Communication of Policies:** Security policies must be clear, accessible, and consistently reinforced. NIST guidance stresses that organizations must define and communicate roles, responsibilities, and expected behaviors so personnel understand how to carry out security functions effectively [31]. Clear communication reduces ambiguity and improves consistency in decision-making.
- **Cross-Departmental Collaboration:** Cybersecurity risk spans technical, operational, and business domains. NIST's Cybersecurity Framework 2.0 highlights governance and organizational coordination as essential for managing risk, emphasizing that cross-functional collaboration improves visibility and accountability [34]. When departments understand how their decisions affect system trust, adherence to security practices improves.

8. Discussion on Technology Interface

User interfaces (UIs) play a crucial role in shaping decision-making and behavior regarding security protocols. Poorly designed interfaces may lead to user error, particularly when security measures are cumbersome or unintuitive. Effective UI design reduces cognitive load, allowing users to navigate security protocols more easily.

For instance, a financial institution that streamlined its login process by reducing the number of required steps significantly decreased failed login attempts. Such adjustments demonstrate how thoughtful design can enhance user experience while improving adherence to security practices [60].

Conversely, organizations must also be cautious of overreliance on technology. Relying solely on automated systems can create a false sense of security, detracting from the necessity of human accountability. Technology can support accountability, but it cannot replace it.

9. Challenges in Measurement

Despite the necessity of measuring accountability, various challenges complicate the process:

- **Data Collection:** Gathering accurate behavioral data is difficult when users hesitate to report incidents, errors, or near misses. Underreporting reduces visibility and distorts risk assessment. NIST emphasizes that organizations should establish processes to support continuous monitoring and encourage timely reporting of security-relevant events, thereby improving risk awareness and decision-making [3]. Reporting culture directly influences data quality.
- **Attribution of Changes:** Linking improvements in security outcomes directly to accountability initiatives is inherently complex. Multiple variables, including technology changes, threat activity, and operational conditions, influence incident rates. NIST notes that risk management decisions must consider uncertainty and multiple contributing factors, reinforcing that outcome attribution requires careful analysis rather than simple correlation [31].
- **Evolving Threat Landscapes:** The threat environment changes continuously, which complicates the use of static metrics over time. New attack methods, tooling, and adversary behavior can shift risk patterns

independently of User Risk. NIST's Cybersecurity Framework 2.0 highlights the need for adaptive risk management and continuous reassessment to maintain alignment with changing threat conditions [34].

10. Strategies for Overcoming Challenges

To effectively measure accountability amidst challenges, organizations may adopt several strategies:

- **Foster a Positive Security Culture:** Open communication and a supportive reporting environment improve both accountability and the quality of measurement data. When users are encouraged to report incidents, errors, and near misses without fear of reprisal, organizations gain more accurate visibility into operational risk. NIST emphasizes that effective risk management depends on organizational culture, defined roles, and clear communication of responsibilities [31]. Culture directly influences whether behavioral data is observable or suppressed. Organizations with mature security cultures demonstrate stronger incident response performance and reduced user-driven risk exposure [23].
- **Use Benchmarking:** Comparing internal metrics against industry standards or peer organizations provides context for evaluating performance. Benchmarking helps distinguish between isolated improvements and meaningful progress relative to external conditions. NIST's Cybersecurity Framework highlights the use of profiles and external comparisons to assess current and target states, enabling organizations to evaluate their cybersecurity posture against recognized practices [34].
- **Continuous Improvement:** Measurement strategies must be regularly reassessed and refined to remain aligned with evolving threats and operational conditions. Continuous monitoring guidance

emphasizes ongoing assessment, feedback, and adjustment as core components of effective risk management [3], [30]. Static measurement approaches degrade over time as environments change. Continuous refinement ensures that accountability metrics remain relevant and actionable.

11. Conclusion

Measuring accountability is essential if organizations want to know whether security expectations are changing behavior. Relevant indicators, practical evaluation methods, and continuous refinement make accountability visible and make improvement defensible.

Closing Leadership Question

What metrics do you use to confirm that accountability in your organization is improving security outcomes?

Part V. User Risk in an Uncertain Future

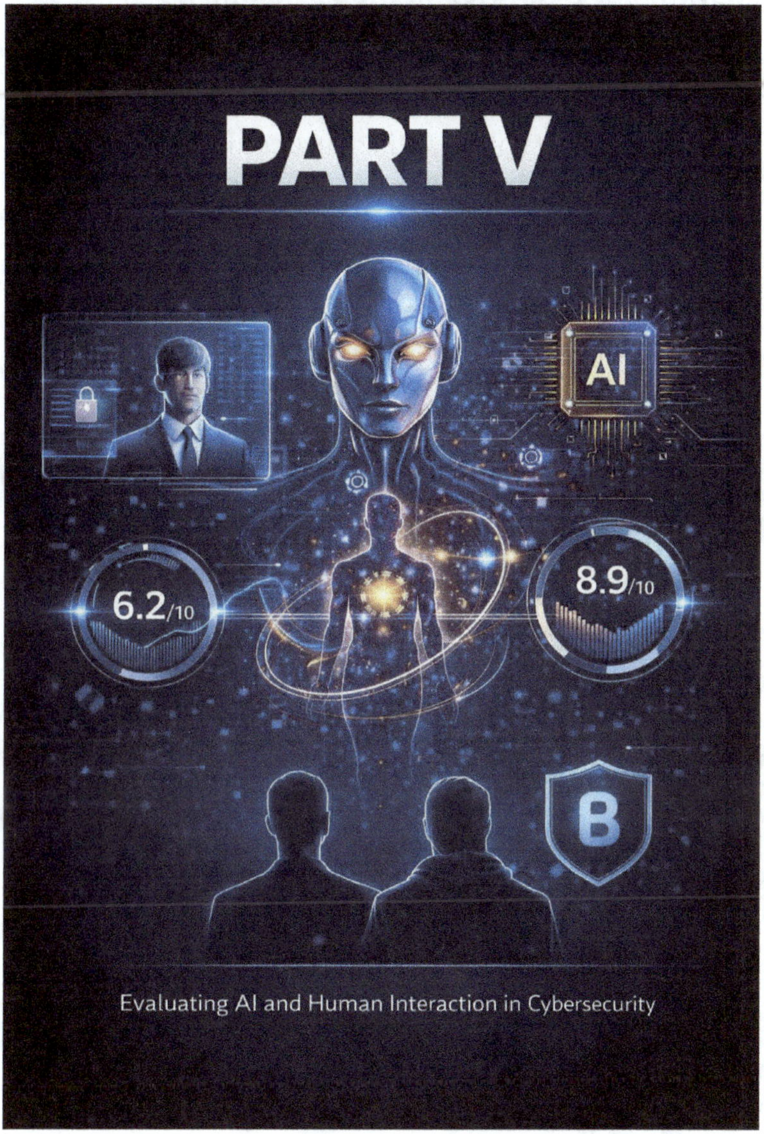

Chapter 12. User Risk in the Zero Epoch

1. Introduction

For decades, cybersecurity has relied on a simple assumption: if cryptographic trust could be established mathematically, digital trust could follow. That assumption is beginning to change.

The concepts developed throughout this book converge in the Zero Epoch. The cybersecurity architecture that protects modern digital systems was established during an era when cryptographic mathematics offered robust assurances of identity, authentication, and confidentiality. Security protocols, certificate authorities, and encryption algorithms crafted a landscape where systems could verify trust relationships with a high degree of mathematical certainty [19].

This foundational assumption significantly influenced the development of cybersecurity frameworks, including the Risk Management Framework (RMF). Controls were designed to ensure that systems implemented secure configurations, protected sensitive data, and authenticated users through cryptographic mechanisms that could be validated and audited. User Risk, defined earlier as the measurable likelihood that human decision variability degrades system trust, control effectiveness, or mission assurance during operational use, becomes more pronounced in the Zero Epoch. In that environment, control validity no longer guarantees trust validity.

Today, however, NIST's finalization of post-quantum cryptographic standards in 2024 and NSA's CNSA 2.0 requirements together mark the formal beginning of a transition period in which current cryptographic assurances can no longer be treated as stable. Advances in quantum computing and artificial intelligence are emerging, posing risks to traditional trust mechanisms. This transition, referred to as the Zero Epoch, signifies the moment when quantum computing achieves the practical capability to compromise widely used cryptographic algorithms that currently secure digital identity and communication. When this threshold is crossed, systems may continue to operate normally while the mathematical foundations supporting identity verification and encrypted communication become increasingly suspect [33], [35].

The implications of this shift extend far beyond cryptography. As automated trust mechanisms wane in certainty, the role of Human Judgment within cybersecurity frameworks grows in significance. Users, administrators, and system owners will increasingly influence how controls function in operational contexts.

The Zero Epoch does not introduce User Risk. It exposes its consequences at scale within environments where traditional trust signals degrade. This chapter explains why that shift makes User Risk measurement more urgent.

2. Cryptographic Trust Before the Zero Epoch

Modern digital systems rely heavily on cryptographic trust. Public-key cryptography and digital certificates help support authentication, integrity, and confidentiality across many operational environments. PKI is the framework for issuing, maintaining, and revoking public-key certificates [7].

Algorithms such as RSA and elliptic-curve cryptography depend on mathematical problems that are computationally difficult for classical systems to solve. As long as those assumptions hold, certificates and digital signatures provide strong evidence of origin and integrity [45].

This cryptographic assurance allows systems to establish trust without constant human verification. When a browser validates a certificate or a system verifies a digital signature, it relies on mathematical proof rather than human interpretation.

3. The Zero Epoch and the Erosion of Cryptographic Certainty

Quantum computing challenges those assumptions. Quantum systems can solve certain classes of problems more efficiently than classical systems, and Shor's algorithm in particular has long been understood as a threat to public-key cryptography based on integer factorization and discrete logarithms [45].

Grover's algorithm presents a separate but related concern for symmetric cryptography. By accelerating the search for encryption keys, it effectively halves the security of symmetric key lengths, meaning that 128-bit keys would offer only 64-bit effective protection against a quantum-capable adversary. Doubling key lengths, such as migrating to AES-256, is the standard mitigation [18].

This does not imply immediate system failure. Authentication may still appear to work. Certificates may still validate. Encrypted sessions may still be established. The concern is that the mathematical guarantees beneath those processes can erode before outward signs of failure are obvious.

NIST's post-quantum cryptography program has now progressed beyond experimentation. In August 2024, NIST announced approval of its first three finalized post-quantum cryptography standards, marking a formal transition point from research to implementation guidance [33]. NSA's Commercial

National Security Algorithm Suite 2.0 likewise states that the updated algorithms will eventually be required for national security systems [35].

These developments reflect a broader reality. The assumptions that historically supported digital trust are no longer stable enough to remain unexamined.

4. Artificial Intelligence and the Manipulation of Trust

Previous chapters discussed behavioral analytics and machine learning as tools for improving visibility into user activity. This section examines those same technologies when deployed adversarially.

Artificial intelligence adds another layer of complexity. AI systems can improve detection, automate analysis, and accelerate incident response. They can also improve the realism and scale of deception.

Generative systems can produce convincing text, voice, and visual material that mimics trusted people and institutions. Deepfake research and security analysis increasingly show how such capabilities can support impersonation, fraud, and social engineering at scale [29].

The problem is not only that AI can deceive. It is that it can replicate trust signals users have historically relied on, including tone, timing, familiarity, and authority.

5. The Convergence of Technologies

The interaction between quantum computing and artificial intelligence is creating a cybersecurity landscape far more intricate than its predecessors. Quantum computing undermines the mathematical foundations of cryptographic trust, while artificial intelligence enhances the sophistication of social engineering and automated deception.

Together, these technologies diminish the reliability of both technical and behavioral trust indicators. A user may receive a message that appears to come from a trusted executive, complete with a valid digital certificate and originating from an authenticated system. Yet, that communication may have actually been generated by an AI system designed to exploit organizational trust relationships.

In such environments, traditional authenticity indicators fail to provide sufficient evidence for confident decision-making [12], [33]. Users must interpret system outputs, verify communications via independent channels, and exercise critical judgment when evaluating requests that could affect system security.

6. The Growing Importance of User Risk

These technological advancements underscore this book's primary argument. Cybersecurity frameworks meticulously measure the implementation of technical controls. The RMF checks to see that controls are correctly implemented, documented, and functioning as intended at the time of authorization.

However, these frameworks seldom measure how human decision variability affects control effectiveness during operational use [2], [42].

While the RMF evaluates the security of systems through technical measures, it falls short of accounting for the Behavioral Variability of the users operating those systems. In the context of the Zero Epoch, this distinction becomes increasingly crucial. As automated trust indicators lose their reliability, human judgment becomes an even more vital factor in maintaining security.

User Risk, therefore, becomes a necessary element of cybersecurity governance. Organizations must assess how behavioral decisions affect control effectiveness in real-world operations.

7. Implications for Cybersecurity Governance

The shift toward the Zero Epoch compels organizations to reevaluate how they measure and manage cybersecurity risk. While technical controls remain essential, ensuring systems implement secure configurations, manage vulnerabilities, and encrypt sensitive information, there is an urgent need to acknowledge that these controls operate within environments influenced by human choices.

Governance processes should include strategies to evaluate behavioral risk. This may involve monitoring privilege usage, assessing approval patterns for exceptions, and analyzing operational decisions that affect system configurations. Training must also evolve. It should not focus solely on recognizing suspicious content. It should also teach users how to validate trust through independent channels, escalation practices, and operational discipline [2].

Organizations should prioritize crypto-agility strategies to enable transition to post-quantum cryptography [33], [35]. Together, these efforts can strengthen resilience in environments where technical and behavioral uncertainties are rising.

8. Conclusion

The Zero Epoch does not diminish the value of cybersecurity frameworks. It reveals the need to broaden how risk is measured within them. As digital systems grow more complex, the relationship between technical controls and human decision-making becomes more consequential.

Understanding and measuring User Risk are crucial steps in preparing for the cybersecurity challenges Zero Epoch entails. The next chapter examines how organizations can measure and govern User Risk within Zero Epoch conditions, building a framework for behavioral accountability that aligns with the governance imperatives identified throughout this book.

Closing Leadership Question

What actions are you taking to ensure human decision-making in your organization reinforces trust as technical assurance declines?

Chapter 13. Measuring User Risk in the Zero Epoch

1. Introduction

The Zero Epoch changes more than cryptography. It changes what organizations must measure to preserve trust. Existing frameworks emphasize technical controls while often overlooking the influence of User Risk on security outcomes [2],[31]. In this environment, understanding and quantifying User Risk becomes essential.

Effective cybersecurity strategies must also consider how variability in human decision-making affects an organization's security posture. While systems can be fortified through robust technical measures, these safeguards can quickly become ineffective because of poor user choices, misinformation, or misinterpretation of trust signals [12],[29].

2. The Importance of User Behavior

User behavior remains a critical variable in control effectiveness. Decisions involving access approval, phishing response, exception handling, and verification can preserve or degrade trust regardless of how well a system is configured.

Large-scale telemetry analysis indicates that identity-based attacks dominate modern intrusion activity, with over 99% of observed attacks targeting password-based authentication and more than 4,000 password attacks occurring per second, underscoring that user authentication practices remain a primary driver of cyber incidents [28].

That reality reinforces the need to treat User Risk as a measurable component of organizational risk rather than as a background assumption.

3. Frameworks for Measuring User Risk

User Risk cannot be measured through a single indicator or technology. Organizations should instead combine several complementary methods that collectively reveal how human decisions influence Operational Trust.

Awareness Training and Education

Regular training remains necessary, but organizations should judge its effectiveness by changes in behavior, not completion alone. Proofpoint's 2023 research demonstrated measurable improvement in phishing reporting rates over time, illustrating that repeated exercises can produce observable behavioral change [40].

Behavioral Analytics

Using analytics to monitor User Risk patterns enables organizations to identify anomalous activity that may indicate potential security incidents. NIST highlights behavioral indicators and anomaly detection as part of continuous monitoring to improve visibility into user actions and emerging threats [3].

Behavioral analytics supports proactive risk management by establishing baseline activity patterns and detecting deviations that may signal misuse, credential compromise, or insider threat activity. Research on insider threat detection further demonstrates that monitoring User Risk over time can reveal precursors to security incidents before they escalate [17].

Behavioral analytics turns user activity from an assumed risk factor into an observable, measurable component of system security.

Feedback Loops

Feedback mechanisms enhance user engagement

and strengthen a security-oriented culture. Encouraging users to report suspicious activities, near misses, and operational challenges improves both situational awareness and organizational learning.

NIST emphasizes that effective risk management requires continuous feedback and communication to refine controls and improve decision-making over time [31], [42]. Feedback loops allow organizations to adapt training, policies, and monitoring strategies based on real-world user experiences, ensuring that security practices remain aligned with operational realities.

4. Integrating User Risk into Cybersecurity Governance

Integrating User Risk into cybersecurity governance requires collaboration among IT, HR, and leadership so that security policies reflect both operational needs and behavioral realities. Developing metrics to assess User Risk can significantly inform organizational strategies, including:

Incident Response Metrics

Monitoring user engagement during security incidents is essential for evaluating how effectively policies are implemented in real-world conditions. Metrics such as detection time, reporting time, escalation behavior, and response coordination provide observable evidence of decision quality during incidents.

NIST emphasizes that organizations must monitor and measure incident response activities as part of continuous monitoring and incident response capabilities, including tracking how events are detected, analyzed, and mitigated [3], [32].

Industry data reinforces the importance of response

maturity. IBM Security reported that organizations with well-developed incident response capabilities and extensive use of security automation experienced breach lifecycle reductions of more than 100 days and significantly lower overall breach costs [20].

These metrics do not simply measure system performance. They measure how users recognize, interpret, and act during security events.

Access Control Reviews

Regular reviews of access permissions and user privileges are critical to reduce exposure to insider threats and limit the impact of credential compromise. Access control effectiveness depends not only on technical enforcement but also on how privileges are assigned, approved, and maintained over time.

NIST requires organizations to enforce least privilege and periodically review access authorizations to ensure users retain only the access necessary to perform their duties [32]. These reviews help identify excessive privileges, orphaned accounts, and inappropriate access patterns.

Verizon's 2023 Data Breach Investigations Report found that stolen credentials and privilege misuse remain among the most common breach vectors, reinforcing the importance of controlling and reviewing user access [52].

Effective access control reviews therefore serve as both a preventive and accountability mechanism by ensuring user permissions align with operational needs and risk tolerance.

5. Fostering a Security-First Culture

Creating a security-first culture requires sustained leadership commitment and consistent reinforcement across the organization. Leaders must model secure behavior, clearly communicate expectations, and integrate security responsibilities into daily operations.

NIST emphasizes that organizational culture, defined roles, and leadership engagement are critical components of effective risk management and governance [31]. Culture influences whether users follow procedures, report issues, and apply sound judgment under pressure [2].

A security-first culture does not eliminate User Risk. It shapes the conditions under which users respond.

Human behavior remains a dominant factor in cybersecurity outcomes. Insider threat analysis shows that negligent User Risk accounts for most internal security incidents, representing about 56% of cases and contributing to an average annual organizational cost exceeding $15 million, demonstrating that non-malicious human actions are a measurable and financially significant driver of cyber risk [39].

6. The Role of Technology in User Risk Management

While User Risk is central to security outcomes, technology plays a critical supporting role in managing User Risk. Advanced capabilities such as machine learning, behavioral analytics, and automated response mechanisms improve visibility into user activity and reduce the time required to detect and respond to threats.

NIST highlights the importance of continuous monitoring, automation, and analytics to detect anomalous behavior and support timely response to security events [3]. These capabilities enable organizations to identify deviations from normal user activity and investigate potential incidents more efficiently.

Industry research continues to show that security AI and automation can materially improve outcomes. IBM Security's 2024 report found that organizations with stronger automation capabilities reduced breach lifecycle duration and improved response efficiency compared with organizations operating with lower automation maturity [21].

Technology enhances decision-making by reducing noise, improving detection accuracy, and accelerating response. It does not replace human judgment. It improves the environment in which that judgment is exercised.

Future Research
Future research should focus on developing quantitative models, behavioral indicators, and validation methods for integrating User Risk into existing risk management frameworks. It should explore standardized methods for quantifying User Risk through behavioral indicators, trend analysis, and risk scoring models. Such approaches may eventually enable organizations to compare user populations, track behavioral risk over time, and incorporate User Risk metrics into authorization decisions.

7. Conclusion

The Zero Epoch increases the cost of leaving User Risk unmeasured. Organizations that integrate User Risk into governance will be better positioned to sustain trust as technical certainty declines.

User Risk cannot be eliminated. It can only be understood, observed, and managed. The Risk Management Framework provides disciplined methods for evaluating systems. The next evolution of cybersecurity governance *must* apply that same discipline to the people who operate them.

The next authorization package you sign will contain evidence of what your systems do. It will reflect months of control implementation, assessment, and documentation. Somewhere in that package, a user population will be represented by training completion percentages and policy acknowledgments. That representation will be treated as sufficient.

You now know it is not. What you do with that knowledge, whether you ask harder questions, document what is unmeasured, or begin building the Behavioral Evidence base your next decision deserves, is where this book ends and your work begins.

Future cybersecurity frameworks will be defined not only by the controls they validate, but by the human behavior they measure.

Closing Leadership Question

What Behavioral Evidence will you require before approving your next authorization decision?

Epilogue: After the Authorization

For decades, cybersecurity programs have measured systems with increasing precision. We count vulnerabilities, track configurations, assess controls, review logs, validate architectures, and document residual risk. We have built disciplined methods for evaluating the technical condition of information systems.

Yet the people who operate those systems are often represented by little more than training records, signed acknowledgments, and access lists.

That is not enough.

This book's central argument is simple. User Risk is not an informal concern, a cultural side issue, or a convenient explanation after an incident. It is a measurable operational variable. Human Judgment can preserve control effectiveness, weaken it, or defeat it entirely. Any risk framework that does not account for that variability presents an incomplete picture of system trust.

This omission matters because authorization decisions carry consequences. Authorizing Officials, CIOs, CISOs, system owners, and security professionals do not sign abstract documents. They accept responsibility for systems that support missions, protect data, enable commerce, deliver public services, and sustain national security. Their decisions depend on evidence. When that evidence excludes the quality of Human Judgment during operations, part of the risk remains hidden.

The examples throughout this book reveal a consistent pattern, and the evidence always appeared convincing.

Configuration baselines were approved. Vulnerability scans were complete. Policies had been acknowledged. Training had been completed. Audit logs were collecting exactly what they were designed to collect. Every dashboard pointed toward compliance. Every assessment supported authorization.

Then came the decision no dashboard could predict. A help desk analyst trusted the wrong caller. An administrator delayed a critical patch. An employee approved a fraudulent authentication request. A security alert was dismissed as another false positive. A vendor account became an attacker's doorway. None of the controls had failed. The people operating within them had reached different conclusions than the architecture expected.

Those outcomes were not anomalies, but human behavior, and they further reflect a weakness in how organizations define and assess Operational Trust.

The Risk Management Framework remains one of the most disciplined approaches available for managing cybersecurity risk. Its structure is not the problem. The problem lies in what it does not yet require organizations to observe directly. RMF provides strong methods for assessing technical safeguards, but it does not explicitly measure whether users consistently make decisions that preserve those safeguards during real-world operation.

Organizations can begin by identifying the decision points where human actions materially affect control performance. Access approvals, privilege changes, exception requests, patch decisions, alert handling, incident reporting, identity verification, and third-party access all represent points where User Risk influences system trust.

The next step is to collect evidence. Training completion can remain part of the record, but it should not stand alone. Organizations should also examine phishing response rates, reporting delays, policy override patterns, privileged access trends, authentication anomalies, exception frequency, and decision quality during exercises or actual incidents. These indicators will not produce a perfect score. No meaningful risk measure does. They will, however, provide better evidence than assumption.

Leaders must also distinguish accountability from punishment. Effective accountability assigns responsibility, establishes expectations, and measures performance. Punishment alone often drives errors and near misses underground. A strong security culture encourages users to report uncertainty, challenge unusual requests, verify identity, and raise concerns before a small decision becomes a major incident.

The Zero Epoch increases the urgency of this work. As artificial intelligence improves deception and quantum computing pressures long-standing cryptographic assumptions, traditional trust signals will become less dependable. Users may confront messages, identities, approvals, and system outputs that appear legitimate but cannot be accepted at face value. In that environment, Human Judgment becomes more important, while also becoming more difficult.

Technical controls will remain essential. They will still enforce boundaries, protect data, detect anomalies, and reduce exposure. But technical validity alone will not guarantee Operational Trust. Systems will depend on people who know when to pause, verify, escalate, challenge, and refuse.

The future of cybersecurity governance will therefore require two forms of assurance.

The first is assurance that technical and administrative controls work. The second is assurance that people use them appropriately and in accordance with policy. Organizations have largely assumed that second form of assurance. It must now be observed.

The work does not require waiting for a new framework, regulation, or control catalog. Organizations can begin within existing governance structures. They can document behavioral assumptions in risk assessments. They can include user-related indicators in continuous monitoring strategies. They can review operational decision patterns during authorization. They can ask whether inherited controls perform consistently across different user populations. They can require evidence that training changes behavior, not merely attendance records.

Most importantly, leaders can ask better questions.

What evidence shows that users preserve system trust during routine operations?

Where do human decisions affect control effectiveness?

Which behaviors remain unmeasured?

What assumptions about judgment are embedded in the authorization decision?

What will leadership require before accepting that risk?

These questions will not weaken the authorization process. They will make it more honest.

Twenty years from now, cybersecurity professionals may look back and wonder why organizations measured every server, vulnerability, configuration, and control while treating human behavior as an assumption. They may find it strange that systems were authorized with extensive technical evidence and minimal Behavioral Evidence, even when incident history repeatedly showed that user decisions shaped outcomes.

The question was never whether User Risk existed. The question was whether we were willing to measure it.

The next generation of cybersecurity governance will be defined by those who answer that question with evidence rather than assumption.

User Risk deserves the same discipline applied to every other material factor in cybersecurity. It should be defined, observed, assessed, governed, and measured over time. Organizations routinely assign quantitative measures to vulnerabilities, assets, control effectiveness, and mission impact.

Human Judgment should be no different. Objective, evidence-based measurement allows leaders to compare risk consistently, monitor changes over time, and make better-informed governance decisions. What matters is not assigning a number for its own sake, but ensuring that the number reflects observable behavior rather than assumption.

This book aims to make that missing variable visible. The responsibility that follows belongs to you.

One day, another authorization package will arrive on your desk. It will contain diagrams, assessments, findings, mitigation plans, and every artifact required to support a risk-based decision. The evidence will be organized. The controls will be documented. The residual risk will appear acceptable.

Then you will sign your name.

From that moment forward, the system's security will no longer depend solely on the controls you approved. It will depend on hundreds, perhaps thousands, of human decisions made long after the authorization is complete.

The question is no longer whether the system is ready. The question is whether the people entrusted with it are.

Appendix. References

[1] AICPA, SOC 2 Trust Services Criteria, American Institute of Certified Public Accountants, 2017. Available: https://www.aicpa.org/resources/article/soc-2

[2] M. Bada, A. Sasse, and J. Nurse, "Cybersecurity awareness campaigns: Why do they fail to change behaviour?" arXiv, 2019. DOI:10.48550/arXiv.1901.02672

[3] NIST, SP 800-137, "Information Security Continuous Monitoring (ISCM) for Federal Information Systems and Organizations," 2011. DOI:10.6028/NIST.SP.800-137

[4] P. Behl and K. Behl, "Cybersecurity Training Using Gamification," Computers & Security, 2022. DOI:10.1016/j.cose.2021.102545

[5] Cybersecurity and Infrastructure Security Agency (CISA), Cybersecurity Performance Goals, DHS, 2023. Available: https://www.cisa.gov/cybersecurity-performance-goals

[6] Cybersecurity and Infrastructure Security Agency (CISA), Colonial Pipeline Ransomware Incident, DHS, 2021. Available: https://www.cisa.gov/news-events/cybersecurity-advisories

[7] NIST, SP 800-57 Part 1 Rev. 5, "Recommendation for Key Management," 2020. DOI:10.6028/NIST.SP.800-57pt1r5

[8] CrowdStrike, Global Threat Report 2024, 2024. Available: https://www.crowdstrike.com/global-threat-report

[9] Cisco Talos, Annual Cybersecurity Report 2024, 2024. Available: https://talosintelligence.com

[10] J. D'Arcy, A. Hovav, and D. Galletta, "User Awareness of Security Countermeasures," Information Systems Research, 2014. DOI:10.1287/isre.2014.0516

[11] U.S. Department of Defense, Cybersecurity Maturity Model Certification (CMMC), 2020. Available: https://dodcio.defense.gov/CMMC

[12] ENISA, Threat Landscape 2023, 2023. Available: https://www.enisa.europa.eu

[13] European Commission, GDPR, 2020. Available: https://gdpr.eu

[14] Federal Trade Commission (FTC), "Equifax Settlement," 2019.

Available: https://www.ftc.gov/enforcement

[15] Google Security Blog, "Security Keys Neutralize Phishing," 2018. Available: https://security.googleblog.com

[16] Google Security Research, "Phishing Study," 2017. Available: https://research.google

[17] F. L. Greitzer and D. A. Frincke, "Insider Threat Detection," IEEE Security & Privacy, 2010. DOI:10.1109/MSP.2010.67

[18] L. Grover, "A Fast Quantum Mechanical Algorithm," STOC, 1996. DOI:10.1145/237814.237866

[19] J. Howell, The Zero Epoch Guidebook, SmartCIO LLC, 2026

[20] IBM Security, Cost of a Data Breach Report 2023, 2023. Available: https://www.ibm.com/security/data-breach

[21] IBM Security, Cost of a Data Breach Report 2024, 2024. Available: https://www.ibm.com/security/data-breach

[22] ISACA, COBIT 2019 Framework, 2019. Available: https://www.isaca.org

[23] ISACA, State of Cybersecurity 2022, 2022. Available: https://www.isaca.org

[26] ISO, ISO/IEC 27001:2022, 2022. Available: https://www.iso.org

[28] Microsoft, Digital Defense Report 2024, 2024. Available: https://www.microsoft.com/security

[29] Y. Mirsky and W. Lee, "Deepfakes," ACM Computing Surveys, 2022. DOI:10.1145/3425780

[30] NIST, SP 800-55, 2011. DOI:10.6028/NIST.SP.800-55

[31] NIST, SP 800-37 Rev. 2, 2018. DOI:10.6028/NIST.SP.800-37r2

[32] NIST, SP 800-53 Rev. 5, 2020. DOI:10.6028/NIST.SP.800-53r5

[33] NIST, Post-Quantum Cryptography Standards, 2024. Available: https://www.nist.gov/pqcrypto

[34] NIST, Cybersecurity Framework 2.0, 2024. Available: https://www.nist.gov/cyberframework

[35] NSA, CNSA Suite 2.0, 2022. Available: https://www.nsa.gov

[36] NVD, "CVE-2017-5638," 2017. Available: https://nvd.nist.gov

[37] OCC, "Capital One Enforcement Action," 2020. Available: https://www.occ.gov

[38] The Open Group, FAIR Risk Standard, 2009. Available: https://www.opengroup.org

[39] Ponemon Institute, Insider Threat Report 2023, 2023. Available: https://www.ponemon.org

[40] Proofpoint, State of the Phish 2023, 2023. Available: https://www.proofpoint.com

[42] K. Parsons et al., "HAIS-Q," Computers & Security, 2017. DOI:10.1016/j.cose.2017.02.002

[43] SANS Institute, Security Awareness Report 2021, 2021. Available: https://www.sans.org

[44] SANS Institute, Security Awareness Report 2023, 2023. Available: https://www.sans.org

[45] P. Shor, "Quantum Computation Algorithms," FOCS, 1994. DOI:10.1109/SFCS.1994.365700

[46] SEC, "Yahoo Breach Disclosure," 2018. Available: https://www.sec.gov

[47] Capital One, "2019 Breach Disclosure," 2019. Available: https://www.capitalone.com

[48] HHS, "Anthem Settlement," 2018. Available: https://www.hhs.gov

[49] DOJ, "Colonial Pipeline Recovery," 2021. Available: https://www.justice.gov

[50] U.S. House Oversight Committee, "Equifax Report," 2018. Available: https://oversight.house.gov

[51] U.S. Senate Committee, "Target Breach Report," 2014. Available: https://www.commerce.senate.gov

[52] Verizon, 2023 Data Breach Investigations Report, 2023. Available: https://www.verizon.com/dbir

[53] World Economic Forum, Cybersecurity Outlook 2024, 2024. Available: https://www.weforum.org

[54] MGM Resorts, "Form 8-K," 2023. Available: https://www.sec.gov

[55] Caesars Entertainment, "Form 8-K," 2023. Available: https://www.sec.gov

[56] K. Starcke and M. Brand, "Decision Making Under Stress: A Selective Review," Neuroscience and Biobehavioral Reviews, vol. 36, no. 4, pp. 1228-1248, 2012. DOI:10.1016/j.neubiorev.2012.02.003

[57] CFPB, "Wells Fargo Enforcement Action," 2020. Available: https://www.consumerfinance.gov

[58] U.S. House of Representatives, "Change Healthcare Hearing," 2024. Available: https://www.house.gov

[59] D. Kahneman, Thinking, Fast and Slow, Farrar, Straus and Giroux, 2011

[60] A. Sasse, S. Brostoff, and D. Weirich, "Usable Security," BT Technology Journal, 2001. DOI:10.1023/A:1011902718709

www.ingramcontent.com/pod-product-compliance
Lightning Source LLC
LaVergne TN
LVHW022227200926
848481LV00006B/2157
* 9 7 9 8 9 9 4 3 8 2 6 3 9 *